# Strengthening Sustainable Investment through International Investment Agreements

OECD

BETTER POLICIES FOR BETTER LIVES

This document, as well as any data and map included herein, are without prejudice to the status of or sovereignty over any territory, to the delimitation of international frontiers and boundaries and to the name of any territory, city or area.

**Please cite this publication as:**
OECD (2024), *Strengthening Sustainable Investment through International Investment Agreements*, OECD Publishing, Paris, https://doi.org/10.1787/a8729c98-en.

ISBN 978-92-64-87689-7 (print)
ISBN 978-92-64-41670-3 (PDF)
ISBN 978-92-64-41854-7 (HTML)
ISBN 978-92-64-95127-3 (epub)

**Photo credits:** Cover © Cristian Lourenço/Getty Images.

Corrigenda to OECD publications may be found at: https://www.oecd.org/en/publications/support/corrigenda.html.

# Foreword

The present Report seeks to clarify the rationale for the inclusion in international investment agreements of new provisions on sustainable investment and to determine how they align with international standards on sustainable investment, identifying areas where a stronger integration of sustainable investment objectives could be pursued. In this exercise, it relies on the principles of the OECD FDI Qualities Recommendation, sets out an ambitious framework based on five key high-level policy principles to which Adherents commit to with a view to strengthening sustainable investment.

This Report was prepared by the OECD Secretariat (Directorate for Financial and Enterprise Affairs, Investment Division) with financial assistance from the European Commission. It was drafted by Alessandra Mistura under the general guidance of Ana Novik (Head of the OECD Investment Division) and Martin Wermelinger (Head of the Sustainable Investment Unit, Investment Division). Rania Amptel-Chafiz and Maria Camila Munoz provided valuable support in the performance of legal and policy research. The Report also benefited from input by Stephen Thomsen, Alexandre de Crombrugghe, Fernando Mistura, Fares Al Hussami, Iris Mantovani, Yasmina Najem, David Gaukrodger, Joachim Pohl, Rima Bugaighis, and Faraz Moosa (all from the Investment Division). Tihana Bule, Froukje Boele, and Marie Bouchard (Responsible Business Conduct Division), as well as Catriona Marshall and Coralie Martin (both from the Development Cooperation Directorate) also provided valuable feedback in the preparation of the Report. Meral Gedik and Lucinda Pearson prepared the Report for publication.

Information for this Report was collected from publicly accessible government sources, in particular legislation, public reports, and official government websites, as well as OECD work in selected countries and other publicly available information by International Organisations.

This Report is developed in the context of the project titled "Integrating principles of FDI Qualities into future investment agreements", implemented with the financial support of the European Commission. The analysis that the Report carries out on treaty language for sustainable investment is not prescriptive and not intended to reflect OECD member states' views. The Report should not be construed as prejudicing or influencing ongoing or future investment treaty negotiations that may be undertaken individually by OECD members or governments that participate in the work on investment at the OECD. It remains understood that the content of each investment treaty should be determined by relevant contracting parties, on the basis of their own policy decisions and different national circumstances.

# Table of contents

## FIGURES



## TABLES



## BOXES

# Abbreviations and acronyms

| | |
|---|---|
| AfCFTA | African Continental Free Trade Agreement |
| ASEAN | Association of Southeast Asian Nations |
| BITs | Bilateral Investment Treaties |
| CETA | Comprehensive Economic and Trade Agreement |
| CFIA | Cooperation and Facilitation of Investment Agreements |
| CSR | Corporate Social Responsibility |
| DEPA | Digital Economy Partnership Agreement |
| EAC | East African Community |
| EC | European Commission |
| EIA | Environmental Impact Assessment |
| EPA | Economic Partnership Agreements |
| ESG | Environmental, Social and Governance |
| ESIA | Environmental and Social Impact Assessment |
| EU | European Union |
| FDI | Foreign Direct Investment |
| FTAs | Free Trade Agreements |
| GEA | Green Economy Agreement |
| IFD | Investment Facilitation for Development |
| IGEC | International Green Economy Collaboration |
| IIAs | International Investment Agreements |
| IPA | Investment Promotion Agency |
| LDCs | Least Developed Countries |
| MNEs | Multinational Enterprises |
| OECD | Organisation for Economic Co-operation and Development |
| PFI | Policy Framework for Investment |
| RBC | Responsible Business Conduct |
| R&D | Research and Development |
| SDGs | Sustainable Development Goals |
| SEA | Strategic Environmental Assessment |
| SIFA | Sustainable Investment Facilitation Agreement |
| SMEs | Small and Medium-Sized Enterprises |
| STEM | Science, Technology, Engineering and Mathematics |
| USMCA | Agreement between the United States of America, the United Mexican States, and Canada |
| WTO | World Trade Organization |

# Executive summary

**International investment agreements (IIAs) are increasingly incorporating new provisions seeking to support sustainable investment.** Initially, these treaties mostly covered investment facilitation understood in its traditional sense, including matters ranging from transparency, exchange of information and streaming of administrative process to the establishment of national focal points to support foreign investors. More recent initiatives have, however, started to address broader measures on which states can rely to improve their own domestic climate for sustainable investment. Provisions of this type have appeared in the context of the negotiation of the World Trade Organization (WTO) Investment Facilitation for Development (IFD) Agreement, the conclusion of the Investment Protocol to the African Continental Free Trade Agreement (AfCFTA) and in the Sustainable Investment Facilitation Agreement (SIFA) between the European Union and Angola, among others.

**While new IIA provisions on sustainable investment have the potential to position foreign direct investment (FDI) more closely with the Sustainable Development Goals (SDGs), it is important to identify the conditions under which their positive effects could materialise**. Harnessing sustainable investment requires a whole-of-government approach, focusing on the adoption of policies that contribute to improving the climate for investment. The OECD (2022) Council Recommendation on Foreign Direct Investment Qualities for Sustainable Development (FDIQR), and the related guidance under the OECD FDI Qualities Policy Toolkit, sets out an ambitious framework, supporting governments in enhancing the impacts of FDI on inclusive and sustainable development. This instrument – which over 50 governments (both OECD and non-OECD members) have already adopted and are actively implementing – can, therefore, provide guidance on how to strengthen the consideration of sustainable investment in IIAs, with special focus not only on investment facilitation but also broader sustainable investment policy considerations.

**The purpose of the report is to clarify the rationale for the inclusion in IIAs of provisions on sustainable investment and to determine how they align with international standards on sustainable investment, identifying areas where a stronger integration of sustainable investment objectives could be pursued**. In this exercise, the report relies on the principles of the FDIQR, as one specific framework – among many existing ones – that seeks to support governments in maximising FDI's contribution to sustainable investment. The FDIQR goes beyond a narrowly understood concept of investment facilitation to examine also other areas – such as the suitability of institutional mechanisms surrounding the investment, the existence of conducive legal and policy frameworks, the availability of technical and financial support, and co-operation with the broader stakeholder community – that can contribute to establishing a domestic climate conducive to sustainable investment.

**The report identifies the potential "added value" of sustainable investment provisions included in IIAs**. First, they might have a "signalling value", insofar as they outline the priorities, objectives, and actions that the treaty parties are willing to pursue in promoting sustainable investment. Alternatively, or in addition, IIA provisions on sustainable investment serve to formalise parties' co-operation on sustainable investment in selected areas, further contributing to the implementation of initiatives that can foster improvements in the domestic investment climate.

**The report also takes stock of IIA provisions on sustainable investment, analysing them against the FDIQR**. The analysis is limited to a sample of nine IIAs, selected based on three criteria (i.e., year of adoption or signature, subject-matter, and type of treaty). The sample includes the Brazil-Morocco Cooperation and Facilitation Investment Agreement (2019), the Modernized Chile-Canada Free Trade Agreement (2019), the Singapore-Chile-New Zealand Digital Economy Partnership Agreement (2020), the Switzerland-Indonesia Bilateral Investment Treaty (2022), the Singapore-Australia Green Economy Agreement (2022), the Investment Protocol to the AfCFTA (2022), the EU-New Zealand Free Trade Agreement (2023), the WTO IFD Agreement (2023) and the EU-Angola SIFA (2023). The analysis finds that sustainable investment provisions in the IIA sample address most FDIQR principles and that, in most cases, the two have similar scope.

**The report identifies areas where IIA provisions on sustainable investment have a narrower scope compared to the FDIQR principles.** Such areas relate to: (i) policy coherence between investment and specific sustainable development-related objectives, especially in connection with gender equality; (ii) the assessment and periodic review of the impacts of investment on sustainable development; (iii) raising awareness on the role that stakeholders can play in supporting sustainable investment; (iv) establishing a closer link between investment promotion activities and sustainable investment; (v) establishing a closer link between investment facilitation activities and sustainable investment; and (vi) ensuring improved consideration of sustainability factors in investment decision making. In all these areas, the report provides examples of domestic practices from selected jurisdictions that can contribute to sustainable investment, clarifying both how states can implement their treaty commitments and address additional sustainable investment-related elements through their treaty-making practice, contributing to the future evolution of their IIAs.

**Based on such a review, the report identifies two modalities, emerging from the IIA sample, on which states can rely to address sustainable investment considerations in IIAs**. A first option relies on the incorporation of substantive language on sustainable investment, potentially resulting in the strengthening of existing treaty commitments on sustainable investment as emerging from the sample of reviewed IIAs. The second option relies on parties' co-operation under the relevant IIAs. The choice of the relevant approach will depend on several elements, including the broader negotiating context, the choice of IIA to be negotiated, and the specific implementation needs of each party. The options discussed are neither prescriptive nor exhaustive. They are only meant to provide an opportunity of reflection to better integrate sustainable investment objectives in IIAs, recognising that there might be alternative and more appropriate options that can still contribute to the strengthening of sustainable investment considerations in IIAs, based on the specific negotiating context.

**The report also introduces an implementation framework to support treaty parties in complying with relevant treaty commitments on sustainable investment**. While treaty parties bear the primary responsibility for the domestic implementation of their international commitments on sustainable investment, their efforts alone might not be enough. The report analyses three mechanisms that can support domestic implementation efforts, and in particular: (i) treaty-based co-operation mechanisms (e.g., joint committees; (ii) partnerships with international organisations; and (iii) development co-operation and international partnerships.

# 1 Context, purpose, and rationale for the research

This chapter provides an overview of the context underlying the research. It focuses, in particular, on recent developments concerning efforts to align international investment agreements (IIAs) with sustainable development, including through the introduction of treaty provisions on investment facilitation. It also briefly examines recent efforts to introduce new provisions in IIAs that seek to facilitate or harness "sustainable investment", as a new category of commitments aligned with the FDI Qualities Recommendation. It then sets out the objectives and structure of the research.

## 1.1. Context

Foreign Direct Investment (FDI) can play a crucial role in achieving the Sustainable Development Goals (SDGs). Through the establishment of long-lasting economic links, foreign investors – including foreign multinational enterprises (MNEs) – can contribute to advancing decarbonisation, enhancing productivity and innovation, creating quality jobs and human capital development, and raising standards of living. (OECD, 2022[1]). Such positive effects can occur both directly and indirectly, through spillover effects, in particular for small and medium enterprises (SMEs). However, FDI's contribution to sustainable development is not automatic. Not only there can be trade-offs among different sustainability objectives, but benefits may also accrue unevenly between and within countries, with some segments of the population being left behind.

Despite the positive role FDI can have to achieve the SDGs and the Paris agreement on climate change, the flows of investment are slowing. Global FDI flows have been suffering a period of stagnation or decline since the Global Financial Crisis of 2008-2009, further dropping by 24% in 2022 (OECD, 2023[2]). Furthermore, multiple compounded crises brought about by the COVID-19 pandemic, growing global geopolitical and trade tensions, and Russia's war of aggression against Ukraine, have all contributed to further shrinking global FDI flows (OECD, 2022[3]). The recent tensions in the Middle East could also likely have a negative impact on global FDI flows.

The materialisation of the contribution that FDI can make to the SDGs rests upon the adoption and implementation of conducive policies at the international and domestic level. The OECD is supporting governments in their efforts to maximise FDI's contribution to sustainable development (Box 1.1). The OECD FDI Qualities Recommendation (OECD, 2022[4]) sets out five key high-level policy principles to which Adherents commit to with a view to strengthening sustainable investment. Building on such principles, the *FDI Qualities Policy Toolkit* (OECD, 2022[1]), together with the *FDI Qualities Indicators* (OECD, 2019[5]), aims to support governments in enhancing the impacts of FDI on inclusive and sustainable development (OECD, 2023[6]). It complements the OECD *Policy Framework for Investment, 2015 Edition* (PFI) (OECD, 2015[7]) by focusing specifically on international investment and providing governments with detailed guidance on how to influence and improve its qualities, beyond investment climate reform.

The FDI Qualities Recommendation recognises that states have a wide variety of policy tools at their disposal to harness sustainable investment, including notably international investment agreements (IIAs). The current report focuses on the role that IIAs can play in harnessing FDI for sustainable development, in particular looking at specific areas related to decarbonisation, gender equality, productivity and innovation, and quality jobs. More specifically, it analyses new treaty provisions that seek to facilitate sustainable investment in the host state, while at the same time addressing broader challenges linked to their implementation at the domestic level and the rationale supporting their inclusion the specific policy instrument represented by IIAs.

### Box 1.1. Harnessing sustainable investment through domestic policies

Ensuring alignment between FDI and sustainable development also rests on the adoption of conducive policies at the domestic level. To help decision makers on how to leverage FDI to promote national development, in 2015 the OECD adopted the updated version of its Policy Framework for Investment (PFI). The PFI provides guidance in 12 policy areas for investment climate reforms that range from the domestic and international legal framework for investment, competition and taxation to green growth and Responsible Business Conduct (RBC) (OECD, 2015[7]). By doing so, it supports the objective of mobilising private investment that supports steady economic growth and sustainable development. In 2022, the OECD also adopted of the OECD (2022[8]) Council Recommendation on the Role of Government in Promoting Responsible Business Conduct, setting out principles and policy recommendations to assist governments, other public authorities, and relevant stakeholders in their efforts to design and implement policies that enable and promote responsible business conduct.

In an effort to further promote the linkages between investment and the SDGs, in 2022 the OECD adopted the OECD FDI Qualities Policy Toolkit. The instrument complements the PFI by providing more detailed and tailored guidance on priorities for policy and institutional reforms to enhance the positive impacts of investment. It focuses, in particular, in four areas of the SDGs, namely: (i) productivity and innovation; (ii) job quality and skills; (iii) gender equality; and (iv) decarbonisation (OECD, 2022[1]). Both the PFI and the FDI Qualities Policy Toolkit are not prescriptive, but rather provide broad policy guidance to improve the impact of FDI on sustainable development. Both documents are based on the assumption that national governments have different priorities, resources, and options at their disposal to harness FDI for sustainable development. As such, they seek to foster a flexible approach that takes into account each country's needs and stage of development.

In 2022, the OECD Council adopted OECD (2022[4]) Council Recommendation on Foreign Direct Investment Qualities for Sustainable Development, based on the PFI and the OECD FDI Qualities Policy Toolkit, and complementing the Recommendation on the Role of Government in Promoting RBC, also adopted in the same year. The FDI Qualities Recommendation is the first multilateral instrument designed to support governments in maximising FDI's contribution to sustainable development. Adherents to the Recommendation commit to a set of five key high-level policy principles in view of attracting sustainable investment:

- **Policy Coherence**: Provide coherent strategic direction on fostering investment in support of sustainable development, and foster policy continuity and effective implementation of such policies.
- **Domestic policies**: Take steps to ensure that domestic policy and legal frameworks support positive impacts of investment on sustainable development.
- **Financial and technical support**: Prioritise sustainable development objectives when providing financial and technical support to stimulate investment.
- **Information and facilitation services**: Facilitate and promote investment for sustainable development opportunities by addressing information failures and administrative barriers.
- **Development co-operation**: Strengthen the role of development co-operation for mobilising FDI and enhancing its positive impact in developing countries.

For each high-level policy principle, the FDI Qualities Recommendation provides more specific guidance to support effective implementation. The detailed set of recommendations, including specific implementation guidance, can be found in Annex A, Supporting Documents (DAF/INV(2024)26/ADD).

### 1.1.1. How international investment agreements incorporated sustainable investment considerations over time

The term "international investment agreements" (IIAs) refers to a wide range of bilateral, regional and multilateral treaties related to foreign investment, as well as the relationship between the host state and the foreign investor, in particular for what concerns the substantive protections afforded to the latter (Wittich, 2017[9]). It includes bilateral investment treaties (BITs), investment chapters of free trade agreements (FTAs), and other treaties with investment provisions, including on investment facilitation.

Despite the general acknowledgement that FDI can contribute to sustainable development, investment treaty practice has only recently started to address sustainable development-related concerns. A 2014 OECD survey of over 2100 IIAs and 1 000 treaty arbitration cases showed that most treaties signed between 2008 and 2013 included references to sustainable development and related issues, such as environmental protection, labour rights, human rights, and anti-corruption. However, such treaties represented only a small part of the reviewed sample (Gordon, Pohl and Bouchard, 2014[10]).

Current investment treaty practice is moving towards the adoption of "new generation" IIAs, which incorporate a wide range of sustainable development-related provisions. A first category considers sustainable development in the context of traditional IIAs provisions. The new language developed can introduce references to sustainable development in the treaty preamble, and the general recognition of the role that FDI can play in its achievement (e.g. Preamble, Morocco-Nigeria BIT; Preamble, Brazil-UAE Cooperation and Facilitation Investment Agreement (CFIA)). It can also seek to safeguard the host state's policy and regulatory space to protect public interests. This can be achieved by introducing "right to regulate" provisions, where states reaffirm their power to adopt measures for the protection of the environment, human and labour rights (e.g. Article 13, Morocco-Nigeria BIT; Article 9, Rwanda-UAE BIT; Articles 8.9 and Article 24, Comprehensive Economic and Trade Agreement between Canada and the European Union and its Member States (CETA); Article 24.3, Agreement between the United States of America, the United Mexican States, and Canada (USMCA)). New language may also include specific carve-outs, exceptions, or clarifications to traditional IIAs provisions, directly reforming "old generation" IIA language. Carve-outs can address, for example, the scope of treaty protection against indirect expropriation (e.g. Article 6.4 Brazil-India CFIA) or the definition of fair and equitable treatment (e.g. Article 5.4, Argentina-UAE BIT).

A second category of provisions introduces new tools and approaches to actively support sustainable investment. Certain IIAs, for example, limit the scope of application of the IIA itself by acting on the definition of "protected investment". They can do so, for example, by clarifying that, to receive protection, an investment must contribute to the sustainable development of the host state (see Article 1, Morocco-Nigeria BIT). More recently, "new generation" IIAs have introduced innovative mechanisms in support of sustainable investment, for example with respect to the upholding of labour standards (e.g. Rapid Response Mechanism under the USMCA). Both categories of sustainable development-related provisions are the main topic of discussion in the OECD's Future of Investment Treaties work, which explores new ways to reform IIAs to align them more closely with sustainable development (Box 1.2).

As to the third category of provisions, an increasing number of treaties seeks to promote sustainable development by incorporating Corporate Social Responsibility (CSR) or Responsible Business Conduct (RBC). This may occur simply through treaty references to existing CSR and RBC standards, including mention of specific instruments such as the OECD Guidelines for MNEs or the United Nations Guiding Principles on Business and Human Rights (e.g. Article 14.17, USMCA; Article 5.2, PACER Plus Agreement; Article 17, Argentina-UAE BIT). In other instances, IIAs set out the conduct that the investor is expected to adopt in the implementation of its investment activities. For example, Brazil's CFIAs include a comprehensive list of investor behaviours addressing human rights compliance, anti-corruption, good governance, and labour and environmental protection (e.g. Article 12, Brazil-India CFIA).

FTAs and Economic Partnership Agreements (EPAs), particularly those involving the European Union (EU), adopt yet another approach to reconcile sustainable development and investment concerns. Starting from 2011, most EU FTAs and EPAs – with the exception of those negotiated with partners in the African, Caribbean and Pacific group of states, which do not currently cover investment – include a specific "Trade and Sustainable Development" Chapter. The Chapter also includes horizontal provisions addressing investment in the host state, including in the form of right to regulate provisions or provisions setting out obligations on states not to lower the level of protection provided in their respective environmental and labour laws and regulations for the purpose of encouraging and attracting trade or investment (e.g. Article 16.2, EU-Japan EPA; Article 19.2, EU-New Zealand FTA). It also sets out provisions that, while not specifically addressing trade or investment, ensure alignment between economic activities and sustainable development, for example by reaffirming obligations deriving from a state's membership to the International Labour Organisation and commitments to effectively implement multilateral environmental agreements to which it is a party (e.g. Articles 16.3 and 16.4, EU-Japan EPA; Articles 19.3 and 19.5, EU-New Zealand FTA), and providing for public consultations and access to information (e.g. Article 22 CETA; Article 16.10, EU-Japan EPA; Article 19.14, EU-New Zealand FTA).

IIAs are not the only international instrument available to align investment and sustainable development objectives. International practice is moving towards the development of new forms of international economic co-operation where sustainable development objectives are put front and centre of the parties' agendas. International Green Economy Collaborations (IGECs) are one example of such "new approaches" to sustainable investment. IGECs can be broadly defined as "international collaborations aimed at achieving mutual environmental and industrial benefits through supporting structural changes in shared value chains" (Aisbett et al., 2023[11]). Contrary to IIAs, where investment represents the parties' main focus, agreements in the form of IGECs seek to foster both economic and sustainability gains at the same time. More specifically, IGECs are focused on actions that generate mutual benefits for both parties, such as the undertaking of joint research projects or co-ordination of climate finance to third parties. One example is the Singapore-Australia Green Economy Agreement (GEA), concluded in 2022. This non-binding agreement sets out a broad collaboration framework between the partners to support economic growth, create jobs in green sectors, promote decarbonisation and mainstream sustainability in national policies and plans. Notably, co-operation in the investment area is only one of the many areas for partners' co-operation, which also include information sharing mechanisms, regulatory co-operation and support for research and development (R&D).

### Box 1.2. Ongoing Treaty Reform Efforts at the OECD

The OECD plays an active role in global efforts to reform IIAs to ensure a greater alignment with sustainable development objectives. Investment treaties are an important component of the framework governing the conditions for foreign investment in many countries. About 2500 such treaties are in force today, including investment provisions of trade agreements. Many of them were designed decades ago with a different global economy and concerns in mind.

The OECD-hosted work programme on the Future of Investment Treaties, launched in March 2021, explores how the investment treaties of tomorrow could help address these challenges and how to deal with existing agreements in a pragmatic way.

The programme comprises two tracks:

- In Track 1, government and non-government participants have initiated the first major sustained multilateral effort to explore how investment treaties factor into climate action. Work under Track 1 focuses on how investment treaties can be drafted and implemented consistent with robust climate action, the Paris Agreement and net zero goals.
- Track 2 considers merits and means to transition substantive clauses of older treaties with designs that are no longer used or are no longer considered satisfactory to newer designs where governments would wish to do so.

### *1.1.2. Emerging focus on facilitating sustainable investment in IIAs*

In parallel with efforts to align IIAs more closely with sustainable development objectives, a limited number of "new generation" IIAs is also starting to incorporate provisions addressing the issue of "investment facilitation for sustainable development". Broadly speaking, investment facilitation can be defined as a "combination of tools, policies and processes that foster a transparent, predictable and efficient regulatory and administrative framework for investment that maximises the benefits to the host economy" (OECD, 2018[12]).

Investment facilitation is distinct from investment promotion, despite their close relationship. The latter concerns, more specifically, the promotion of "a country or a region as an investment destination", while the former is about making it easy for investors to establish or expand their existing investments (OECD, 2015[7]). The two also target different beneficiaries. Investment promotion is primarily directed towards new investors that have yet to make their investment decision, while facilitation mostly addresses investors that have already made their investment choices and are moving into the establishment phase.

Investment facilitation is an ongoing activity that takes place throughout the life of the investment project, from establishment to operation. Notably, investment facilitation can consist of:

- Supporting investors in navigating the policy and regulatory framework applicable to the investment (e.g. through one-stop-shops, information portals for foreign investors, business registration portals etc.).
- Adopting and implementing policies to improve transparency, predictability, and effectiveness in the investment environment (e.g. through streamlining administrative procedures, ensuring that the regulatory framework is clear and transparent, establishing good governance mechanisms).
- Implementing relevant institutional processes in an impactful manner (e.g. by relying on inter-agency co-ordination, public-private dialogues, and capacity building for public officials).

Many of the tools, policies and processes that fall under the umbrella of investment facilitation are already considered as key components of the PFI and FDI Qualities Initiatives that allow states to harness sustainable investment at the domestic level.

In recent years, the consideration of the role that investment facilitation can play in achieving sustainable development has moved from the domestic to the international level, resulting in the inclusion of relevant provisions in IIAs. Such a change is occurring even though investment facilitation remains firmly rooted in measures undertaken at the domestic level, thus raising profiles from the perspective of implementation of relevant treaty commitments. The trend concerning the incorporation of investment facilitation provisions in IIAs has also undergone a shift over time. Initially, IIAs mostly focused on investment facilitation *per se*, without any express linkage with sustainable investment. In this context, they mostly addressed matters ranging from transparency, exchange of information and streamlining administrative process to the establishment of national focal points to support foreign investors, or general provisions on the improvement of the business environment in the host state.

One example of this approach may be found in Brazil's CFIAs. The Brazilian approach represents a decisive shift in paradigm in investment negotiation. Rather than being solely focused on traditional investment protection provisions, the CFIAs focused on attracting and retaining investment through activities of co-operation and facilitation (Skartvedt Guven, 2020[13]). In particular, Brazilian CFIAs often include some of the following obligations:

- Encourage investments through co-operation and facilitation activities (e.g. Article 3.2, Brazil-India CFIA).
- Develop a common investment co-operation and facilitation agenda through the Joint Committee established under the agreement (e.g. Articles 13.4 and 25, Brazil-India CFIA; Articles 18.4 and 26, Brazil-Ecuador CFIA; Articles 18.4 and 26, Brazil-Guyana CFIA; Articles 18.4 and 26, Brazil-Suriname CFIA; Articles 17.4 and 25, Brazil-Ethiopia CFIA). Such an agenda often includes topics such as the freedom of movement of key personnel linked to the establishment and the operation of the investment, the streamlining of administrative processes, and the implementation of technical exchange and co-operation activities (e.g. Annex I, Brazil-Malawi CFIA).
- Ensure the transparency and dissemination of information relevant for the investors of the other party, including on the regulatory environment and business opportunities in the host state (e.g. Article 17, Brazil-India CFIA; Article 9, Brazil-Ethiopia CFIA).
- Establish or appoint of national focal points to support investors of the other party in their activities in the host state (e.g. Article 14, Brazil-India CFIA; Article 18, Brazil-Ethiopia CFIA; Article 19, Brazil-Ecuador CFIA).
- Apply regulatory measures affecting the investment in a reasonable, objective, and impartial manner (e.g. Article 10. Brazil-Chile CFIA).

Notably, the investment facilitation measures envisaged in Brazilian CFIAs have a rather general nature, without being specifically linked to sustainable development outcomes.

More recently, new IIAs have started to stress the importance of investment facilitation for the achievement of sustainable development outcomes. Exemplary in this sense is the negotiation of the World Trade Organization (WTO) Investment Facilitation for Development (IFD) Agreement. The negotiation process concluded in July 2023, and resulted in a comprehensive text agreement addressing traditional issues on investment facilitation, such as transparency of investment measures, streamlining of administrative processes relating to investment activities, domestic regulatory coherence, and international co-operation between home and host states (World Trade Organization, 2023[14]). The WTO IFD Agreement also includes a specific chapter on "Sustainable Investment", addressing RBC and anti-corruption. The agreement is notable as it is the first WTO treaty that includes an express reference to RBC and the OECD Guidelines for Multinational Enterprises.

The adoption of the WTO IFD Agreement is the culmination of an ongoing process that sees the incorporation of investment facilitation provisions in an increasing number of IIAs, including investment chapters of FTAs and regional investment agreements. At the regional level, investment facilitation provisions appear in the recently adopted Investment Protocol to the African Continental Free Trade Agreement (AfCFTA). The Protocol also addresses traditional issues linked to transparency, streamlining of administrative processes, and provision of aftercare services. However, it also includes provisions directly tackling facilitation of sustainable investment, especially in connection with the granting of incentives to foreign investors (see Articles 7-10, Investment Protocol to the AfCFTA). Similar provisions also slowly making an appearance in other "new generation" IIAs (e.g. Article 9.20, PACER Plus; Articles 8, 18 and 22, Intra-MERCOSUR Investment Cooperation and Facilitation Protocol; Article 10.17, Regional Comprehensive Economic Partnership Agreement).

Investment facilitation, specifically directed towards harnessing sustainable investment, is also a key priority in EU's investment policy agenda. In 2019, the EU's amended negotiating directives for EPAs with partner countries in the Africa, the Caribbean and the Pacific region mentioned establishing a framework that will "facilitate, enhance and stimulate mutually beneficial sustainable investment" between the parties, taking into account multilateral initiatives on investment facilitation. In October 2019, the EU started negotiations with five Eastern and Southern Africa partners (so-called ESA-5: Comoros, Madagascar, Mauritius, Seychelles and Zimbabwe) to deepen the existing Economic Partnership Agreement (European Union, 2020[15]), and provisions on investment facilitation largely inspired by the WTO IFD Agreement are being negotiated as a part of this deepened EPA. More recently, in its Trade Policy Review of 2021, the European Commission (EC) announced that it would pursue new generation "sustainable investment agreements" with interested partner countries in Africa and the Southern Neighbourhood, once again with specific focus on investment facilitation (European Commission, 2021[16]).

Such efforts led to the conclusion, in November 2023, of the EU's first Sustainable Investment Facilitation Agreement (SIFA), negotiated with Angola (European Commission, 2023[17]). The EU-Angola SIFA adopts an ambitious approach to investment facilitation and sustainable development. The agreement addresses traditional areas generally pertaining to investment facilitation, such as transparency and predictability, focal points, and streamlining of authorisations procedures. It also includes a specific chapter dedicated explicitly to "investment and sustainable development". Here, it addresses the general alignment between investment activities with labour and environmental concerns and sets out specific obligations for the parties to facilitate investment in a way that contributes to sustainable development objectives, including gender equality and decarbonisation. In this sense, the EU-Angola SIFA represents another concrete attempt at the international level to align investment facilitation and sustainable development and to pursue sustainable investment (see Box 1.3 for an assessment of the OECD's work on the EU-Angola SIFA in selected Southern Neighbourhood countries).

## 1.2. Implications and rationale of IIA provisions on sustainable investment

Provisions such as those included in the WTO IFD Agreement, the Investment Protocol to the AfCFTA and the EU-Angola SIFA are notable in that they are – explicitly or implicitly – aimed at fostering sustainable investment in the host state. They are distinct from traditional "sustainable development" provisions in IIAs, as they require the host state to take active measures aimed at improving the domestic investment climate for the specific purpose of harnessing sustainable investment. They are also broader than traditional "investment facilitation" provisions, as investment facilitation is only one component of the broader set of measures that the host state has at its disposal to improve domestic investment climate.

The introduction of such new category of "provisions on sustainable investment" within the IIA system represents a recent development, whose implications have not yet been fully analysed. Their inclusion in IIAs rests on the assumption that they have the potential to support sustainable FDI. However, it is essential to identify the conditions under which their positive effects could materialise. In turn, this requires addressing different, but related issues.

First, it is necessary to determine what "provisions on sustainable investment" means in the context of IIAs. The brief analysis carried out above has shown that the concept has been expanding over time, moving beyond the narrow boundaries of traditional IIA provision on "investment facilitation". Ongoing discussions in international fora, including the OECD, have highlighted how investment facilitation is only one – admittedly important – step in harnessing sustainable investment. Other elements, such as policy coherence, investment incentives, and conducive legal frameworks, are all equally critical and necessary. In this sense, the OECD Recommendation on Foreign Investment Qualities for Sustainable Development offers a comprehensive list of policy tools that states can use to strengthen their domestic climate for sustainable investment. Notably, the FDI Qualities Recommendation also recognises the key role that IIAs can play in this respect and highlights the importance of aligning such instruments with sustainable investment objectives.

Second, it is important to stress that the modalities – i.e. the policy tools and approaches – that states can use to support sustainable investment vary considerably and have all a pre-eminently domestic dimension. In fact, the implementation of treaty commitments on sustainable investment will necessarily require the implementation of relevant measures at the domestic level. Conversely, what states are already doing domestically to support sustainable investment may also influence treaty design at the domestic level. As such, the analysis of IIA provisions on sustainable investment cannot be separated from the analysis of relevant domestic practices.

Third, the issue of the overall rationale for inclusion in IIAs of provisions on sustainable investment will need to be clarified. It should be first noted that the inclusion of sustainable investment provisions in IIAs will not necessarily lead to increased sustainable investment. In fact, the overall potential of IIAs to generate benefits for both home states and host states alike has never been established with full certainty (Pohl, 2018[18]). The added value of IIA provisions on sustainable investment must then be found elsewhere. A first possible answer might lie in the "signalling value" of such provisions, insofar as they outline the priorities, objectives, and actions that the treaty parties are willing to pursue in harnessing sustainable investment. Alternatively, or in addition, IIA provisions on sustainable investment also serve to formalise parties' co-operation on sustainable investment in selected areas. In this sense, they provide a framework for the establishment of co-operation initiatives, exchanges of best practices, capacity building and technical assistance on sustainable investment.

In both cases, the possibility for such "added value" to materialise is subject to a key condition. Any positive effect that could potentially arise from IIAs with respect to the achievement of sustainable investment is strictly dependent on the effective implementation of treaty commitments at the domestic level. In the absence of effective implementation, IIAs commitment on sustainable investment will be ultimately meaningless. Hence, any analysis concerning the scope and rationale of new IIA provisions on sustainable investment will necessarily involve a discussion on the practical modalities to implement such provisions at the domestic level.

## 1.3. Purpose of the report

Against this background, the research will seek to clarify the rationale for the inclusion in IIAs of provisions on sustainable investment. It will also determine how recent IIAs incorporating such type of provisions align with international standards on sustainable investment, identifying areas where a stronger alignment could be pursued. In this exercise, the research will rely on the principles of the FDI Qualities Recommendation and related instruments, which provide an ambitious framework supporting governments seeking to maximise FDI's contribution to sustainable investment. Such an approach allows looking beyond a narrowly understood concept of investment facilitation and expand the analysis to other areas – such as the suitability of institutional mechanisms surrounding the investment, the existence of conducive legal and policy frameworks, the availability of technical and financial support, and co-operation with the broader stakeholder community – that can contribute to establishing an investment climate conducive to sustainable investment.

The research will also analyse domestic practices in selected areas in line with sustainable investment objectives that can contribute to the domestic implementation of international commitments, as well as tools and mechanisms that can support effective domestic implementation. It will also assess how sustainable investment principles as enshrined in the FDI Qualities Recommendation and current domestic practices on sustainable investment may influence the negotiation of future IIAs, with a view to ensuring a stronger alignment between investment and sustainable development objectives.

### Box 1.3. Towards more sustainable investment frameworks

The OECD in co-operation with the EC assessed the extent to which the legal, regulatory and institutional frameworks for investment in selected Southern Neighbourhood countries – namely, Algeria, Egypt, Jordan, Morocco and Tunisia – are aligned with the objectives, requirements and key investment facilitation standards enshrined in the EU-Angola SIFA. By providing a gap analysis of investment facilitation shortcomings in the selected Southern Neighbourhood, the project aims at guiding the EC and the Southern Neighbourhood partners on potential future SIFA negotiations.

A new OECD report provides a stocktaking of the current investment climates of the selected Southern Neighbourhood countries, benchmarked against investment facilitation standards reflected in the EU-Angola SIFA. In particular, the report reviews the state of readiness of each of the selected Southern Neighbourhood countries in light of the SIFA's key facilitation standards, based on an assessment of their respective domestic legal and regulatory frameworks and institutional arrangements for investment. More specifically, the report outlines and describes the key facilitation standards enshrined in the EU-Angola SIFA, relating specifically to the transparency and predictability of domestic regulatory frameworks and the streamlining of investment authorisation procedures, and how these standards are reflected in each of the selected countries, by way of legal, regulatory and institutional channels.

The report identifies potential room for improvement in the selected Southern Neighbourhood countries and underlines the extent to which each of their domestic frameworks align with the EU-Angola SIFA's key facilitation standards, with a view to guide the EC and interested partners in the region on potential future SIFA negotiations. Strengthening Southern Neighbourhood's investment facilitation frameworks could help countries not only attract more FDI, but also harness its potential positive benefits.

Source: (OECD, 2024[19])

A few additional remarks are necessary at this stage before proceeding further.

First, it is acknowledged that IIAs are not the only instrument that governments are using to foster sustainable investment. Such a consideration also emerges from the FDI Qualities Recommendation, which recognises that states have a wide range of policy options and tools at their disposal from which they can chose in their efforts to align investment and sustainable development priorities. States retain both the power to prioritise among the policy tools and instruments available as well as among the sustainable development objectives to be achieved. At the same time, the increasing attention that new-generation IIAs have themselves placed on sustainable investment underscores how the alignment between investment and sustainable development is becoming a key priority in investment treaty-making practice. The current research, therefore, builds on this trend, reflecting how one specific policy instrument – that is IIA – can be harnessed for sustainable investment.

Second, even when considering IIAs as a specific policy tool, it is important to recall that this is by no mean a unitary category. IIAs are heterogeneous and can take the form of "traditional" protection-focused BITs, FTAs with a wide variety of chapters – including investment, environment, labour, and sustainable development – and broader treaties with investment-related provisions, notably investment facilitation agreements such as the EU-Angola SIFA and the WTO IFD Agreement. Investment-related provisions can also be included in new types of international arrangements, such as IGECs with non-binding nature. All these instruments have different structures and objectives, which will inevitably influence the type of provisions that they include and the extent to which they align with sustainable investment objectives.

Lastly, it is important to stress that efforts to clarify the scope and rationale of sustainable investment provisions in IIAs are complementary to ongoing reform processes to more closely align IIAs with sustainable development. Issues concerning how to align investment treaties with the Paris Agreement and net zero goals or how to redesign substantive clauses of older treaties in a way that is conducive to the achievement of the negotiating parties' objectives are, however, the specific topic of discussion in existing international fora. As such, they will not be specifically discussed in the current research.

## 1.4. Structure of the report

The current report is structured as follows:

- Chapter 2 reviews selected provisions of a small sample of IIAs and multilateral initiatives on sustainable investment to assess their alignment with the principles of the FDI Qualities Recommendation and identify areas that could offer opportunities for a stronger alignment of future IIAs with sustainable investment objectives.
- Chapter 3 identifies examples of domestic practices in selected countries or regions that are conducive to the FDI Qualities Recommendation. The consideration of such domestic practices is important, as IIAs provisions will ultimately need to be implemented at the domestic level. Domestic review may offer additional insights on potential commitments that could be transposed at the international level to inform future practice.
- Chapter 4 examines the issue of the domestic implementation of international commitments, developing a novel "Implementation Framework" seeking to guide the actions of state parties to the IIA at the domestic level.
- Chapter 5 analyses two examples of approaches on which states rely to address sustainable investment objectives in the context of the IIAs negotiation. Such approaches neither prescriptive nor exhaustive. They are only meant to provide an opportunity of reflection to better integrate sustainable investment objectives in IIAs.

## References


Aisbett, E. et al. (2023), "International green economy collaborations: Chasing mutual gains in the energy transition", *Energy Research & Social Science*, Vol. 104, p. 103249, https://doi.org/10.1016/j.erss.2023.103249. [11]

European Commission (2023), *EU and Angola conclude first-ever Sustainable Investment Facilitation Agreement*, https://ec.europa.eu/commission/presscorner/detail/en/IP_22_6136. [17]

European Commission (2021), *Trade Policy review – An Open, Sustainable and Assertive Trade Policy*, COM(2021) 66 final, https://eur-lex.europa.eu/resource.html?uri=cellar:5bf4e9d0-71d2-11eb-9ac9-01aa75ed71a1.0001.02/DOC_1&format=PDF. [16]

European Union (2020), *Council Decision (EU) 2020/13 of 19 December 2019 amending the negotiating directives for the negotiation of Economic Partnership Agreements with the African, Caribbean and Pacific countries and regions*, https://eur-lex.europa.eu/legal-content/EN/TXT/PDF/?uri=CELEX:32020D0013. [15]

Gordon, K., J. Pohl and M. Bouchard (2014), "Investment Treaty Law, Sustainable Development and Responsible Business Conduct: A Fact Finding Survey", *OECD Working Papers on International Investment*, No. 2014/1, OECD Publishing, Paris, https://doi.org/10.1787/5jz0xvgx1zlt-en. [10]

OECD (2024), *Towards More Sustainable Investment Frameworks: Evaluating the Feasibility of Sustainable Investment Facilitation Agreements with Southern Neighbourhood Countries*, OECD Publishing, Paris, https://doi.org/10.1787/411468b9-en. [19]

OECD (2023), *FDI in Figures, April 2023*, https://www.oecd.org/daf/inv/investment-policy/FDI-in-Figures-April-2023.pdf. [2]

OECD (2023), *Policy Toolkit for Strengthening FDI and SME Linkages*, OECD Publishing, Paris, https://doi.org/10.1787/688bde9a-en. [6]

OECD (2022), *FDI Qualities Policy Toolkit*, OECD Publishing, Paris, https://doi.org/10.1787/7ba74100-en. [1]

OECD (2022), *International investment implications of Russia's war against Ukraine*, OECD Publishing, Paris, https://doi.org/10.1787/a24af3d7-en. [3]

OECD (2022), "Recommendation of the Council on Foreign Direct Investment Qualities for Sustainable Development", *OECD Legal Instruments*, OECD/LEGAL/0476, OECD, Paris, https://legalinstruments.oecd.org/en/instruments/OECD-LEGAL-0476. [4]

OECD (2022), "Recommendation of the Council on the Role of Government in Promoting Responsible Business Conduct", *OECD Legal Instruments*, OECD/LEGAL/0486, OECD, Paris, https://legalinstruments.oecd.org/en/instruments/OECD-LEGAL-0486. [8]

OECD (2019), *FDI Qualities Indicators: Measuring the sustainable development impacts of investment*, OECD Publishing, Paris, https://doi.org/10.1787/0894dfba-en. [5]

OECD (2018), "Towards an international framework for investment facilitation", *OECD Business and Finance Policy Papers*, No. 47, OECD Publishing, Paris, https://doi.org/10.1787/b82771dc-en. [12]

OECD (2015), *Policy Framework for Investment, 2015 Edition*, OECD Publishing, Paris, https://doi.org/10.1787/9789264208667-en. [7]

Pohl, J. (2018), "Societal benefits and costs of International Investment Agreements : A critical review of aspects and available empirical evidence", *OECD Working Papers on International Investment*, No. 2018/1, OECD Publishing, Paris, https://doi.org/10.1787/e5f85c3d-en. [18]

Skartvedt Guven, B. (2020), *Briefing Note: Investment Promotion and Facilitation for Sustainable Development*, Columbia Center on Sustainable Investment, https://ccsi.columbia.edu/sites/default/files/content/docs/publications/Briefing-Note-Investment-Promotion-and-Facilitation-for-Sustainable-Development-FINAL.pdf. [13]

Wittich, S. (2017), "International Investment Law", in *The Practice of Shared Responsibility in International Law*, Cambridge University Press, https://doi.org/10.1017/9781316227480.033. [9]

World Trade Organization (2023), *WTO Structured Discussion on Investment Facilitation for Development - Statement by the Co-Ordinators*, https://docs.wto.org/dol2fe/Pages/SS/directdoc.aspx?filename=q:/INF/IFD/W51.pdf&Open=True. [14]

# 2 Assessing international investment agreements against the principles of the FDI Qualities Recommendation

This chapter analyses selected provisions on sustainable investment derived from a sample of nine international investment agreements (IIAs), assessing them against the principles of the FDI Qualities Recommendation (FDIQR). This chapter describes the methodological framework guiding the stocktaking exercise. Then it takes stock of the scope, tools and approaches that IIA provisions adopt to pursue sustainable investment, comparing them against the FDIQR to identify those areas with a narrower, similar, or broader scope and those where the FDIQR is not addressed. Lastly, it identifies areas that offer an opportunity for further consideration of sustainable investment elements, in alignment with the FDIQR.

## 2.1. Methodology

The FDI Qualities Recommendation (FDIQR) enshrines a set of policy principles with a view to strengthen the sustainable impact of investment. Such principles are divided into four categories: (i) policy coherence; (ii) domestic policies; (iii) technical and financial support; (iv) information and facilitation services; and (v) co-operation and partnerships. The FDI Qualities Policy Toolkit supports governments in identifying priorities for domestic policy and institutional reform to strengthen the sustainable impact of investment, providing practical examples for the implementation of the FDIQR principles. Due to the focus placed on sustainable investment beyond narrow investment facilitation, these instruments are particularly suitable to act as baseline against which existing international investment agreements (IIAs) that include sustainable investment elements can be compared.

The FDIQR dedicate a specific principle to IIAs, recognising the need to align IIAs with sustainable investment objectives, "including by ensuring appropriate domestic policy space and social dialogue to achieve these objectives". More broadly, the FDIQR also calls for coherence between IIAs and other existing international obligations relating to specific sustainable development areas, including decarbonisation, gender equality, quality jobs and innovation. Understood in this sense, the FDIQR recognises the key importance of ongoing reform efforts to more closely align IIAs with sustainable development concerns and the Paris Agreement, such as those ongoing under the OECD-hosted work programme on the Future of Investment Treaties.

At the same time, new provisions on sustainable investment raise specific challenges, as they effectively call for the adoption at the domestic level of a wide range of measures seeking to support sustainable investment. Notably, such measures are expressly considered under the FDIQR principles, albeit outside of the specific IIA context. The issue therefore arises of how to reconcile specific FDIQR principles addressing what are essentially domestic measures to IIAs, as specific policy instruments of international nature. This exercise includes an element of discretionary choice, as it relies on the interpretation of the FDIQR. This needs to be taken into count when interpreting the results of the analysis. It also requires the development of a methodological framework that allows understanding and interpreting IIAs through the lens of the FDIQR.

The methodological framework is firmly grounded in the FDIQR and the principles it sets out to harness sustainable investment, both generally and in connection with specific sustainability goals – namely: (i) productivity and innovation; (ii) job quality and skills; (iii) gender equality; and (iv) decarbonisation. The methodological framework sets out the criteria that justify benchmarking an IIA provision against a specific principle in the FDIQR. For each principle of the FDIQR (identified through reference to its number and short title), Table 2.1 identifies the criteria justifying the consideration of an IIA provision under a certain principle. Annex B, Supporting Documents (DAF/INV(2024)26/ADD) sets out the full methodological framework for the assessment of IIA provisions against the FDIQR principles, also outlining the criteria under which a specific IIA provision would be considered as relevant for the achievement of the specific sustainability goals identified above.

## Table 2.1. Reconciling the FDIQR principles and IIAs

| Category | No. | Title | Criteria for IIA consideration under a specific FDIQR principle |
|---|---|---|---|
| Policy coherence | 1.a | National strategies and plans | Treaty references to strategies and plans addressing investment and/or areas relevant for sustainable development objectives considered in the FDIQR. |
| | 1.b | Inter-agency co-ordination | Treaty references to the establishment or operationalisation of inter-agency mechanisms at the national or subnational level aimed at fostering co-ordination on investment and/or areas relevant for sustainable development objectives considered in the FDIQR. |
| | 1.c | Inclusive decision making | Treaty references to the establishment, strengthening, or operationalisation of stakeholders' consultation mechanisms and processes relating to the adoption of investment-related policies, strategies, laws, and regulations as well as to the implementation of FDI projects. |
| | 1.d | Impact assessment | Treaty references to the implementation of impact assessment processes relating to the adoption and review of investment-related policies, strategies, laws, and regulations, as well as the implementation of FDI projects (e.g. Environmental Impact Assessments). |
| Domestic policies | 2.a | Alignment with the OECD Policy Framework for Investment (PFI) | Treaty references to strengthening and improving the main features of existing legal and policy frameworks for investment in alignment with selected provisions of the OECD Policy Framework for Investment, looking in particular at transparency, integrity and rule of law, prevention of corruption, and quality regulation.[1] |
| | 2.b | Domestic alignment | Treaty references to domestic measures (i.e. laws, regulations, and policies) that are conducive to the achievement of the sustainable development objectives considered in the FDIQR. |
| | 2.c | International alignment | Treaty references to international treaties and standards on sustainable development objectives considered in the FDIQR, such as the ILO Conventions or multilateral environmental agreements.[2] |
| Financial and technical support | 3.a | Incentives for policy goals | Treaty references to financial, technical, and regulatory incentives contributing to the achievement of sustainable development objectives considered in the FDIQR. |
| | 3.b | Incentives transparency | Treaty provisions addressing the dissemination of information on incentives for policy goals and their regular review by governmental entities. |
| Information and facilitation services | 4.a | Awareness raising | Treaty references to activities of awareness raising on sustainable investment and/or sustainable development objectives relating to areas considered in the FDIQR. |
| | 4.b | Investment promotion | Treaty references to investment promotion activities. |
| | 4.c | Investment facilitation | Treaty references to investment facilitation activities.[3] |
| | 4.d | Promoting Responsible Business Conduct (RBC) | Treaty references to international instruments on RBC, including, but not limited, to the OECD Guidelines on Multinational Enterprises, the United Nations Guiding Principles on Business and Human Rights, and the ILO Declarations. |
| | 4.e | Sustainability factors in FDI decisions | Treaty references to environmental, social and governance (ESG) issues that can guide the decision on whether to undertake an investment project or not. |
| Co-operation and partnerships | 5.a | Technical assistance and capacity building | Treaty references to the provision of technical assistance and/or capacity building to a party, contributing to the achievement of sustainable development objectives. |
| | 5.b | Development co-operation | Treaty references to the alignment of donor support and beneficiaries' national priorities on investment and sustainable development. |
| | 5.c | Multi-stakeholder partnerships | Treaty references to the establishment of co-operation and dialogue mechanisms between the parties and other stakeholders. |

1. The analysis does not include PFI areas relating to investment protection, competition, taxation, intellectual property, public procurement, and consumers protection. Promotion of responsible business conduct (RBC) falls under Recommendation 4.d.
2. Relevant international treaties and standards do not include international standards on RBC, as enshrined in the OECD Guidelines and other instruments (e.g. United Nations Guiding Principles on Business and Human Rights).
3. These references are related to investment facilitation understood in a narrow sense, focusing on the creation of a transparent, predictable and efficient regulatory and administrative framework for investment (OECD, 2018[1]).

### 2.1.1. Identifying a selected sample of IIAs

Provisions addressing sustainable investment have become increasingly common in IIA over recent years, and particularly since 2015 (UNCTAD, 2023[2]). However, due to the number of provisions involved, a mapping and stocktaking exercise of all IIAs addressing sustainable investment would be beyond the scope of this exercise. This paper limits the analysis to a sample of selected IIAs based on three criteria:

- *Temporal*: Only IIAs signed or adopted in the past five years (2019 to 2023) are covered limiting the analysis to the most recent practice.
- *Subject-matter*: Only IIAs that contain provisions on sustainable investment are included. These are understood in their broadest scope, i.e. to include the compendium of policies and measures that contribute to improving the domestic climate for investment, in line with the FDIQR and the OECD Policy Framework for Investment (PFI).
- *Type of treaties*: To provide a balanced representation of the variety of IIAs in current practice, the sample draws from four different types of treaties, namely: (i) bilateral investment treaties (BITs); (ii) selected chapters of deep free trade agreements (FTAs) addressing Investment, Trade and Sustainable Development, chapters having specific cluster-level relevance (e.g., Gender, Small and Medium-sized Enterprises, Energy), and chapters addressing investment facilitation-related provisions (e.g., Good Governance and Regulatory Practices); (iii) regional and plurilateral IIAs; and (iv) new-generation agreements tackling specific sustainability issues, including by addressing investment. It is understood that the type of treaty will influence the amount and type of provisions on sustainable investment that the treaty may include.

Accordingly, the research will focus on a sample of nine IIAs, listed in Figure 2.1.

Figure 2.1. IIA sample

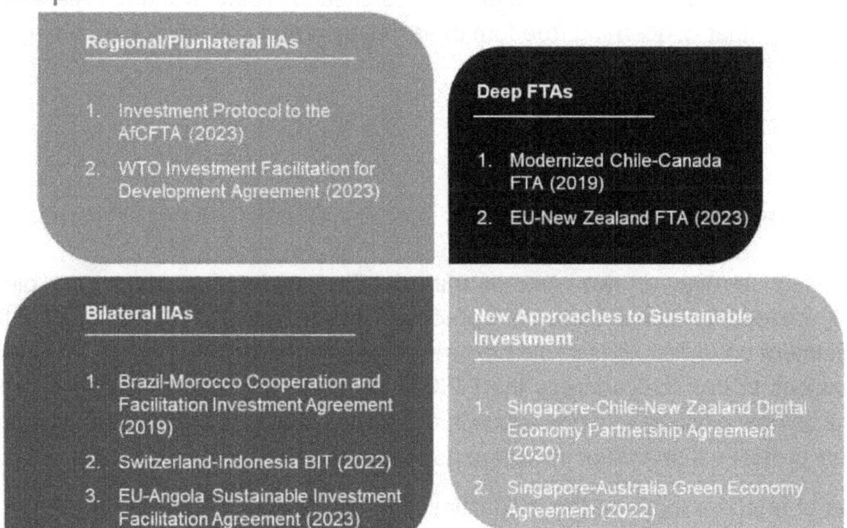


Note: The figure highlights the agreements that are part of the IIA sample. For FTAs, the research will focus only on specific chapters, although the research could be further expanded in the future through the assessment of provisions found in additional chapters.
Source: OECD.

It is understood that the IIA sample, and the treaties included therein, is not exhaustive and that there are additional IIAs that also meaningfully contribute to sustainable investment, including through the introduction of innovative tools and approaches (Box 2.1). The limitation in the sample size is nevertheless necessary to keep the scope of the research clearly manageable and defined. At the same time, the analysis below can still be useful to highlight emerging approaches to sustainable investment in IIAs, identifying potential areas that could be subject to further developments.

### Box 2.1. Treaties outside of the IIA sample contributing to sustainable investment: The case of the United States-Mexico-Canada Agreement

The United States-Mexico-Canada Agreement (USMCA), signed in 2018 and entered into force in 2020, provides heightened consideration to sustainable investments concerns. The USMCA includes provisions typically found in new-generation IIAs, including aimed at preserving the state's right to regulate to ensure that investment activities are carried out "in a manner sensitive to environmental, health, safety or other regulatory objectives" (Article 14.16). In addition, it also adopts innovative approaches that can actively contribute to sustainable investment, in alignment with the principles of the FDIQR. Such approaches include, among other things:

- Encouraging – compatibly with the parties' own legal system – the recourse to flexible and voluntary mechanisms (e.g., auditing and reporting, sharing of information and expertise, public-private partnerships) to protect the environment and natural resources (Article 24.14);
- Setting out a best effort obligation on the parties to facilitate and promote investment in environmental goods and services, with a view to contributing to green growth and encouraging sustainable development (Article 24.24);
- Promoting co-operation to increase investment opportunities for small and medium-sized enterprises (SMEs), including owned by under-represented groups, with a view to promoting the exchange of information and best practices and facilitating SMEs' access to international markets (Article 25.2);
- Setting out binding obligations on the parties concerning the adoption of measures to prevent and combat bribery and corruption (Articles 27.1 and ff); and
- Establishing a Rapid Response Mechanism designed to protect workers in case that their labour rights, in particular concerning freedom of association and collective bargaining, are violated in specific facilities (Annex 31-A).

Source: OECD based on the text of the USMCA.

### *2.1.2. Describing the methodology*

The stocktaking exercise relies on two types of analysis. First, it identifies which principles of the FDIQR receive no or only limited attention in current IIA practice. This provides a first indication of the areas where sustainable investment considerations could be strengthened in future IIA practice. This exercise includes counting of provisions in IIAs that address the FDIQR. By itself, this type of analysis cannot be used to draw conclusions on how existing IIAs provisions in the sample address sustainable investment in line with the FDIQR. It only provides a snapshot on where gaps may exist.

The second type of analysis looks at the modalities with which the FDIQR and the provisions of the IIA sample address sustainable investment concerns. The exercise focuses on the content of the obligation enshrined in the relevant IIA provision (i.e. its subject-matter) comparing it with the content of the relevant principle under the FDIQR. On this basis, it assigns a grade from one (1) to three (3) in accordance with the scale below:

1. **Narrow scope**: The relevant IIA provision makes a general reference to an objective of the FDIQR but falls short on prescribing policy tools to achieve it.
2. **Similar scope**: The relevant IIA provision addresses both the policy objective to be achieved and the policy tools to be used, in line with the FDIQR.
3. **Broader scope**: The relevant IIA provision mentions the policy objective to be achieved and introduces specific policy tools that are not envisaged in the FDIQR.

The analysis allows to identify the areas where future IIA practice could go further, through reference to either additional policy tools and approaches mentioned in the FDIQR and not considered in the IIA sample or to specific policy tools enshrined in the IIA sample but not addressed in the FDIQR. The inclusion of such novel tools and approaches, however, will depend on the identification of the rationale justifying their inclusion in future IIA practice.

The degree of correspondence between an IIA provision and the content of a specific FDIQR principles may be also influenced by the legal nature of the provision itself – that is, its intensity. The "intensity" criterion is concerned with the legal nature of the obligation and, in particular, its binding force. As much as a provision may have a similar scope to the FDIQR from a subject-matter perspective, its contribution to sustainable investment will be much more limited if it is lacking a binding force. The analysis of each IIA provision will, therefore, need to consider how the provision is drafted, and in particular whether it falls under one of the following categories:

- **Declaratory provisions**: they only reaffirm the parties' existing rights or commitments under prior international agreements.
- **Permissive provisions**: they reaffirm the parties' prerogative to undertake a certain action ("*may*") if they wish to do so.
- **Exhortative provisions**: they encourage parties to act in a certain manner ("*should*") but without imposing any binding obligation to do so.
- **Best effort provisions:** they set out the parties' obligation to adopt measures for the achievement of a certain objective but without requiring that the objective is effectively achieved (e.g. "*shall endeavour*").
- **Provisions of result**: they set out the parties' obligation to achieve a specific result through a specific conduct (*"shall"*).

It is understood that the results of the analysis are subject to changes based on potential revisions to the methodological framework, which may affect the interpretation of relevant treaty provisions and correspondence with FDIQR principles. In addition, the analysis is based exclusively on the text of the relevant treaty provisions. It does not consider issues linked to the actual impact of treaty provisions. The relative novelty of provisions on sustainable investment – in particular appearing in more recent treaties such as the WTO IFD Agreement or the EU-Angola SIFA –and the ensuing lack of data availability, makes such an assessment impossible to perform at this stage.

## 2.2. Analysing the IIA sample against the principles of the FDIQR

The stocktaking exercise entails a review of selected provisions in the IIA sample to assess if and how they address the principles of the FDIQR. The exercise analyses a total of 396 provisions from the IIA sample, by applying the methodological framework for alignment between FDIQR principles and IIAs. It focuses, in particular, on IIA provisions that address sustainable investment. This is understood in its broadest sense, i.e. as a compendium of policies and measures that can contribute to improving the domestic climate for investment, in line with the FDIQR and the OECD PFI. The review does not cover IIA provisions addressing investment protection or market access, which is the subject of ongoing OECD work on IIA reform, in particular under the "Future of Investment Treaties" Work Programme.

As a first step, the analysis counts IIA sample provisions that address FDIQR principles (Figure 2.2). When a treaty provision falls under the scope of more than one FDIQR principle, both primary and secondary – and, in limited cases, tertiary – correspondence is noted. The purpose of this exercise is simply to show which principles of the FDIQR are not addressed in the IIA sample, and where gaps may therefore exist. However, it does not allow to draw conclusion on how IIA sample provisions address the FDIQR principles.

The analysis shows that, based on the current formulation of the methodological framework, provisions in the IIA sample address most of the FDIQR principles. One notable exception is FDIQR principle 1.a on the development and promotion of investment-related strategies and plans coherent with sustainable development objectives, which does not find any correspondence in the IIA sample.

**Figure 2.2. Correspondence between IIA sample and FDIQR principles**

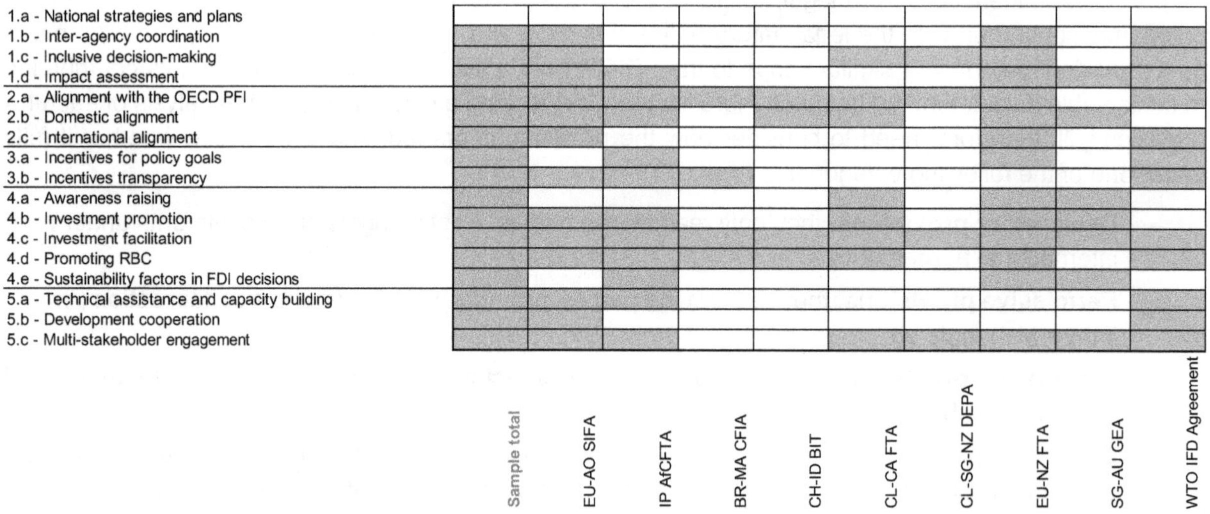


Note: The figure shows which FDIQR principles are addressed in the IIA sample and in specific treaties within the IIA sample. A treaty is deemed as addressing an FDIQR principle if it includes at least one provision that meets the criteria set out in the methodological framework. The level of alignment between the relevant provision and the underlying FDIQR principle is not relevant for the purpose of determining the correspondence. The figure shows that provisions in the IIA sample address most of the FDIQR principles, with one exception represented by FDIQR principle 1.a.
Source: Data from the sample of 9 selected IIAs.

Other principles only find limited attention in the IIA sample. This is the case, for example, for FDIQR principle 4.a on awareness raising on impacts of investment on sustainable development, which finds a mention in only three (3) treaties within the IIA sample – namely, the Chile-Canada FTA, the EU-New Zealand FTA and the Singapore-Australia Green Economy Agreement (GEA). FDIQR principle 1.b on inter-agency co-ordination, FDIQR principle 3.a on incentives for policy goals, and FDIQR principle 4.e on sustainability factors in FDI decisions also find limited attention in the IIA sample. More specifically, only the EU-Angola SIFA, the EU-New Zealand FTA, and the WTO Investment Facilitation for Development (IFD) Agreement address FDIQR principle 1.b on inter-agency co-ordination. FDIQR principle 3.a on incentives for policy goals is addressed in the Investment Protocol to the African Continental Free Trade Agreement (AfCFTA), the EU-New Zealand FTA and the WTO IFD Agreement, while FDIQR principle 4.e on sustainability factors in FDI decisions is regulated only under the Investment Protocol to the AfCFTA, the EU-New Zealand FTA and the Singapore-Australia GEA.

The stocktaking exercise also focuses on the IIA sample alignment with four sustainability areas considered under the FDIQR, and namely: (i) productivity and innovation; (ii) job quality and skills; (iii) gender equality; and (iv) decarbonisation (Figure 2.3). The results show that certain treaties within the IIA sample – and in particular the EU-Angola SIFA, the EU-New Zealand FTA, and the Investment Protocol to the AfCFTA – provide comprehensive attention to all four sustainability areas under the FDIQR. Other treaties, instead, prioritise certain sustainability areas over others, although almost all – with the exception of the WTO IFD Agreement – are explicitly concerned with issues linked to labour rights and the creation of quality jobs.

Looking at the data from the perspective of the individual treaties within the IIA sample, it is possible to note that the consideration given to the FDIQR principles varies depending on the underlying treaty. Some, like the EU-Angola SIFA, the EU-New Zealand FTA, or the WTO IFD Agreement, address almost all FDIQR principles. In others such as the Brazil-Morocco CFIA and the Switzerland-Indonesia BIT, instead, consideration is provided to only a limited number of FDIQR principles. Such a conclusion is not surprising. Indeed, the level of correspondence between an IIA and the FDIQR principles will depend also on the nature, scope, and objectives of the IIA itself. Treaties such as the Brazil-Morocco CFIA and the Switzerland-Indonesia BIT pursue very specific and targeted objectives. As such, it is to be expected that the consideration they give to FDIQR principles will also be more limited. On the contrary, IIAs like the EU-Angola SIFA or the WTO IFD Agreement look at sustainable investment more holistically, thus leading to a more widespread integration of FDIQR principles.

## Figure 2.3. Correspondence between IIA sample and FDIQR sustainability areas

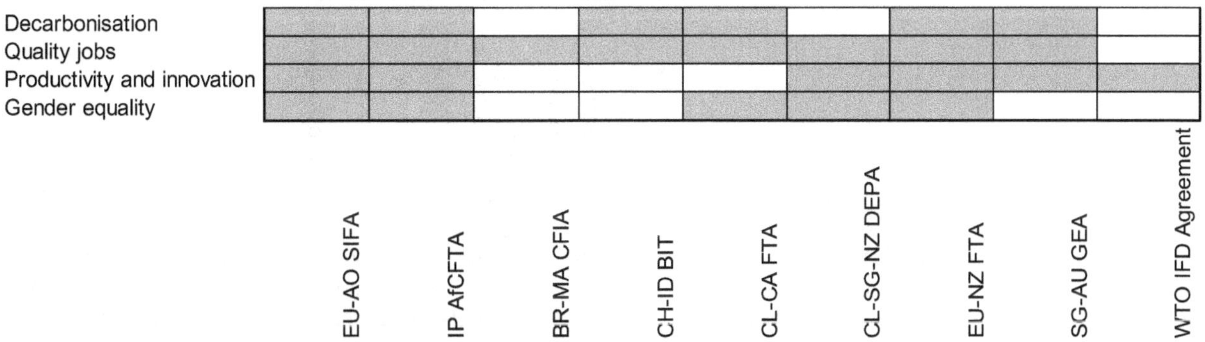


Note: The figure shows which FDIQR sustainability areas are addressed in specific treaties within the IIA sample. A treaty is deemed as addressing an FDIQR sustainability area if it includes at least one provision that meets relevant criteria under the methodological framework. The figure shows that only a limited number of treaties within the IIA sample address all the sustainability areas considered in the FDIQR, with most remaining focused only on quality jobs.
Source: Data from the sample of 9 selected IIAs.

This correspondence-based stocktaking exercise does not say anything about how IIA sample provisions address the principles of the FDIQR. This assessment can be done only through the application of a specific subject-matter scale, seeking to determine whether the relevant provision has narrower scope compared to the FDIQR principles, a scope similar to the corresponding FDIQR principle, or if it goes beyond the FDIQR and the policy tools it envisages to harness sustainable investment (Figure 2.4).

In general, all treaties within the IIA sample contain one or more provisions with a similar scope to the FDIQR principles from a subject-matter perspective. Limited exceptions relate to FDIQR principle on awareness raising, where the limited number of IIA sample provisions on this topic simply refers to the importance of raising awareness on specific sustainable development-related issues without providing any guidance or identifying specific policy tools on how to do so. Certain treaties within the IIA sample also have a more similar scope to the FDIQR principles than other IIAs, offering opportunities to shape future practice. For example, all IIA sample treaties have a similar scope to the FDIQR when it comes to traditional investment facilitation measures like transparency of investment information and streamlining of administrative procedures. However, only certain IIAs within the sample create a stronger alignment between investment promotion and facilitation activities and the specific sustainability areas under the FDIQR, in alignment with FDIQR principles 4.b and 4.c.

**Figure 2.4. Subject-matter analysis of the IIA sample against the FDIQR principles**

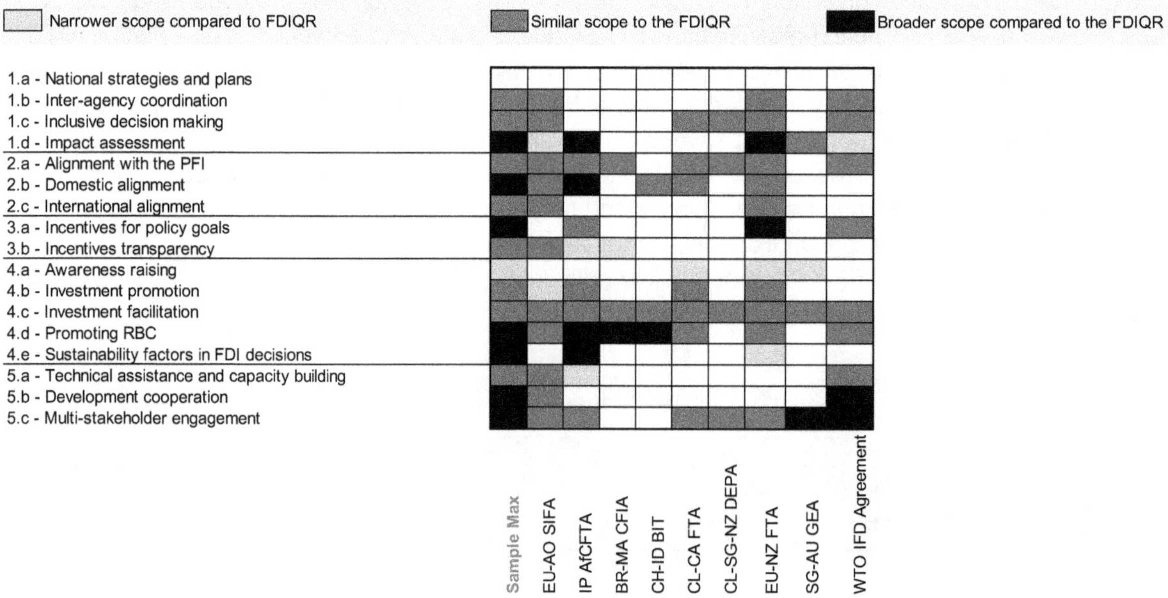


Note: This table shows the subject matter comparison between the FDIQR principles and the IIA sample, as well as specific treaties within the IIA sample. It does so by applying a subject-matter scale that shows how the scope of provisions within the relevant treaties compares to the FDIQR principles, and in particular whether they have a narrower, similar or broader focus. The figure shows that provisions in the IIA sample are generally aligned with the principles of the FDIQR, although there are areas where relevant provisions have a narrower (e.g. awareness raising) or broader (e.g. consideration of sustainability factors in FDI decisions) scope. Please note that the results of the analysis are subject to changes based on revisions and amendments to the methodological framework.
Source: Data from the sample of 9 selected IIAs.

There are also treaties within the IIA sample that seem to have a broader scope compared to specific FDIQR principles, when introducing policy tools not discussed therein. For example, the Investment Protocol to the AfCFTA appears to go beyond the scope of the FDIQR principles when it refers to the local content measures to align investment and sustainable development, and when the Investment Protocol to the AfCFTA, the Brazil-Morocco CFIA or the Switzerland-Indonesia BIT introduce specific investor obligations. Both the Investment Protocol to the AfCFTA and the EU-New Zealand FTA provide more precise criteria guiding the assessment of FDI's impacts on sustainable development, beyond the current scope of FDIQR principle 1.d on impact assessment and periodic review. While these provisions may offer suggestions of additional sustainable investment-related elements that could be considered through future IIAs and the FDIQR, their usefulness and desirability will have to be carefully assessed.

## 2.3. Reflections for further integration of IIAs and the FDIQR principles

Based on the high-level overview of the IIA sample, compared against the FDIQR principles, the stocktaking exercise identifies three main areas that offer opportunities for reflection on additional sustainable investment areas, in line with the FDIQR principles, that states might decide to address through their IIAs:

1. Areas where IIA sample provisions do not address, or only narrowly address, tools and practices in line with the FDIQR principles.
2. Areas where IIA sample provisions introduce tools and practices in line with the FDIQR principles that can strengthen the consideration of sustainable investment.
3. Areas where IIA sample provisions introduce tools and practices beyond the scope of the FDIQR principles.

Table 2.2 shows the full list of the identified areas. The detailed analysis of IIA sample provisions falling under each category is set out under Annex C, Supporting Documents (DAF/INV(2024)26/ADD), with main findings summarised below.

The table also shows that not all FDIQR principles are considered in the analysis. For example, only a limited number of treaties in the IIA Sample address FDIQR principle 1.b on inter-agency co-ordination. However, they do so in a manner that is already contributing to sustainable investment, in line with the FDIQR principles. The possibilities to consider additional elements in this area, therefore, are more limited. The full analysis of IIA sample provisions falling under the scope of FDIQR principles and not providing possibilities for further development is set out under Annex D, Supporting Documents (DAF/INV(2024)26/ADD).

Table 2.2. Potential areas to strengthen the sustainable impact of IIAs based on the FDIQR principles

| Areas not or narrowly addressing FDIQR principles | Areas in line with FDIQR principles | Areas going beyond FDIQR principles |
|---|---|---|
| FDIQR principle 1.a: National strategies and plans | FDIQR principle 1.d: Impact Assessment | Local content measures |
| FDIQR principle 3.a: Incentives for policy goals | FDIQR principle 2.b: Domestic alignment | Investor obligations |
| FDIQR principle 4.a: Awareness raising | FDIQR principles 4.b and 4c: Investment promotion and facilitation | |
| FDIQR principle 4.e: Sustainability factors in FDI decisions | FDIQR principle 4.d: Promotion of RBC | |

### *2.3.1. Areas where the IIA sample does not address, or narrowly addresses, FDIQR principles*

#### *FDIQR principle 1.a: National strategies and plans*

FDIQR principle 1.a encourages national strategies and plans on investment, growth, innovation, jobs and skills development, gender equality, decarbonisation and regional development to be as coherent as possible (OECD, 2022[3]).

While generally referring to the importance of policy coherence in specific sustainable development-related areas, treaties within the IIA sample do not specifically address FDIQR principle 1.a. None of the provisions examined expressly calls for the integration of sustainable development concerns in national investment strategies and plans at the level of detail expected under the FDIQR. For example, to achieve decarbonisation objectives, FDIQR principle 1.a encourages national strategies and plans to set out clear and specific environmental and decarbonisation targets, identify the resources and tools to achieve them, and provide for performance indicators to measure progress over time. In the gender area, FDIQR principle 1.a recommends mainstreaming gender considerations into investment promotion strategies and plans, to ensure that efforts to attract FDI to specific sectors or regions do not exacerbate existing inequalities.

The implementation of FDIQR principle 1.a, however, is grounded in choices related to the allocation of domestic resources, the definition of clear action plans and targets and the definition of monitoring and evaluation frameworks. Given the specificity in the implementation of this FDIQR principle, which will depend on the actual institutional context in the negotiating parties, the principle might not be adequately addressed in international instruments such as IIAs. Parties could, however, include a reference to national strategies and plans in existing provisions addressing the need for coherence between investment policies and sustainable development-related objectives.

### *FDIQR principle 3.a: Incentives for policy goals*

FDIQR principle 3.a addresses the specific types of assistance – including financial and technical incentives – that states can use to pursue specific sustainability goals linked to decarbonisation, productivity and innovation, job quality and gender equality.

Given the variety of measures that states can adopt to support sustainable development-related policy goals, the limited provisions in the IIA sample do not address the principle in a comprehensive manner. The approach adopted in certain treaties – such as the Investment Protocol to the AfCFTA – is to first reaffirm in general the parties' power to introduce incentives to pursue sustainable development. The treaty then also provides for a non-exhaustive list of financial and technical assistance measures that the parties may introduce, including in connection with specific areas, such as low-carbon investment (Article 8, Investment Protocol to the AfCFTA). Another approach is to address specifically only certain types of incentives that can facilitate the achievement of targeted sustainable development objectives, such as technology transfer, local suppliers' development, and decarbonisation (see Article 25, WTO IFD Agreement; Article 19.11(2), EU-New Zealand FTA; Articles 29-30, Investment Protocol to the AfCFTA).

Decisions on incentives are essentially a domestic matter and depend on the party's own priorities and resources. As such, the matter might not be comprehensively regulated in an IIA context. Current practice in the IIA sample already ensures alignment with FDIQR principle 3.a. In fact, provisions listing existing examples of incentives or highlighting specific incentives that can contribute to achieve targeted goals may provide a useful indication as to what the parties consider as "sustainable investment" to be pursued in an IIA setting. In addition, IIAs may contribute to fostering co-operation in the areas of incentives. Such a co-operation could be directed, in the first instance, to improving policy coherence in the field. For example, it could focus on the identification of which incentives should be allowed to pursue specific sustainable development objectives, thus also reducing risks of conflicting incentive regimes. Co-operation could also be directed at enhancing parties' capacity to comply with treaty provisions addressing incentives, in particular concerning their periodic review. In this context, they could support the implementation of initiatives aimed at strengthening domestic capacity on reporting and assessment on the incentives' impacts on the desired sustainability goal.

### *FDIQR principle 4.a: Awareness raising*

FDIQR principle 4.a addresses the need to raise stakeholder awareness on the impacts of their consumption and investment choices, in particular with respect to the specific areas of decarbonisation and gender equality.

Treaty references to awareness raising in the IIA sample are broadly absent and often have a narrower scope compared to FDIQR principle 4.a. In the gender area, existing provisions in the EU-New Zealand FTA (Article 19.4.4) and in the Chile-Canada FTA (Article Nbis-01.7) only address awareness raising on "gender equality laws, regulations, policies and practices". However, they fail to consider the impacts on gender stereotypes and discrimination resulting in reduced access to opportunities for women, in line with the FDIQR. In the decarbonisation area, instead, the EU-New Zealand FTA (Article 19.11.5) treats awareness raising as secondary concern in provisions addressing investment promotion and facilitation, which can be implemented also through public education campaigns. The Singapore-Australia GEA (paragraph 9.g.v), instead, implicitly refers to awareness raising when addressing the partners' co-operation with ecolabelling organisation.

Given the importance of awareness raising in aligning sustainable development and investment outcomes, states wishing to putt a stronger focus on related activities in line with FDIQR principle 4.a may rely on different options. A first approach could be to build on existing provisions. Alternatively, or in addition, they could decide to focus on co-operation, for example through the development between the parties of joint awareness raising initiatives, addressing decarbonisation and gender. In this respect, future IIAs could provide additional indications as to potential activities – such as public information campaigns, or public-private policy dialogues – that the parties could pursue, in line with FDIQR principle 4.a.

### *FDIQR 4.e: Sustainability factors in FDI decisions*

FDIQR principle 4.e concerns the need for investors, both financial and operational, to consider sustainability factors – that is, environmental, social and governance (ESG) concerns – when making investment decisions.

There are only limited references to this principle in the IIA sample. Environmental factors sometimes appear among the criteria that should guide decisions on investment, often in conjunction with the consideration of available technical and scientifical information or the application of the precautionary approach (see Article 19.13, EU-New Zealand FTA; Article 34.1(d), Investment Protocol to the AfCFTA). In other cases, IIA sample provisions address the need for voluntary disclosure and sustainability schemes (see Article 19.11.1, EU-New Zealand FTA; Article 39.4, Investment Protocol to the AfCFTA). The Singapore-Australia GEA is notable in this regard, as it sets out a framework for the partners' co-operation on (i) the strengthening of ESG ecosystem in their respective countries, "to improve decision-making by businesses and investors" (paragraph 9.c.vii); and (ii) the development of robust global climate-related financial disclosures and reporting standards (paragraph 9.c.viii). Co-operation in these areas is essential. FDIQR principle 4.e recognises that the lack of consistency and comparability in ESG reporting standards is one of the main issues that the FDIQR identifies as negatively affecting the effectiveness of non-financial disclosure measures.

States wishing to expand consideration of sustainability factors in IIA in line with FDIQR principle 4.e could consider building on efforts ongoing in international fora to further foster the parties' regulatory and technical collaboration on the development and uptake of clear, comparable, and proportionate ESG frameworks and metrics that contribute to sustainable investment.

## *2.3.2. Areas where the IIA sample can strengthen consideration of sustainable investment, in line with the FDIQR principles*

### *FDIQR principle 1.d: Impact Assessment*

FDIQR principle 1.d relates to the assessment of FDI's impacts on sustainable development through a variety of processes, and namely: (i) the impact assessment of investment-related policies, laws, regulations, or investment projects; and (ii) the periodic review of the adopted measure or the authorised project. It also tackles FDI's potential positive contribution to productivity and innovation, gender equality, decarbonisation, and quality jobs through reliance on adequate monitoring and evaluation frameworks.

Several treaties in the IIA sample address FDIQR principle 1.d on impact assessment and periodic review, to a different extent. Among all, the regime set out in the EU-New Zealand FTA is particularly noteworthy. After reaffirming the parties' commitment to perform an impact assessment and periodic review of major measures of general application, the treaty sets out the criteria that regulatory authorities shall apply when conducting such exercises. For impact assessment (Article 22.8.2), these include the consideration of whether a regulatory measure is needed in the first place, what options are available that would allow a party to achieve the same policy objective without the need to regulate, and what are the potential social, economic and environmental impact of the options. As such, it specifically requires the assessment of environmental and social impacts, including on decarbonisation, labour issues and SMEs development. For periodic review (Article 22.9.1 and 22.9.2), relevant criteria include the consideration of more efficient alternatives and whether the current measure is still adequate considering the objective to be achieved. It further provides that, in the impact assessment and periodic review of measures aimed at protecting the environment or labour conditions and potentially entailing adverse consequences on investment, parties shall take into account available scientific and technical information and apply the precautionary approach (Article 19.13). Lastly, the EU-New Zealand FTA also goes further than other treaties in the IIA sample by setting out an obligation for the parties to ensure that their own domestic legislation provides for the implementation of an environmental impact assessment (EIA) for energy or mining projects having significant impact on the environment (Article 13.8.1).

Examples in the IIA sample on monitoring and evaluation are scarce. The only treaty that briefly discusses the issue is the Singapore-Australia GEA, which identifies data measurement, statistical capacity, and development of indicators and data tracking tools as some of the areas on which partners will co-operate (paragraph 9.g.vii). By doing so, parties can contribute to ensuring that monitoring and evaluation activities are grounded in reliable and comparable data. Partners' co-operation extends also to the exchange of measurements and reporting and verification in carbon accounting mechanisms, with a view to building trust in the carbon market (paragraphs 9.d.ix and 9.d.x).

Additional sustainable investment-related elements that states could decide to address through IIAs potentially include criteria for impact assessment and periodic review, including through reference to available scientific and technical information. States could also decide to strengthen the intensity of relevant obligations, by turning the hortatory language into obligations of result. This exercise, however, will have to be carried out with caution, as the potential suspension of the investment project at the conclusion of the EIA process could expose the state to liability in case it was to amount to a breach of investment protection provisions potentially enshrined under the relevant IIA or other existing BITs. Lastly, parties may decide to address monitoring and evaluation directly in IIAs, either in the form of collaboration for the development of relevant frameworks and indicators – as done, for example, in the Singapore-Australia GEA – or through provisions referencing the need for parties to apply such frameworks in their impact assessment and periodic review exercises.

### *FDIQR principle 2.b: Domestic alignment*

FDIQR principle 2.b addresses the issue of policy coherence by requiring alignment between domestic policy frameworks with sustainable investment objectives. In general, treaties within the IIA sample achieve a good level of alignment with FDIQR principle 2.b, especially when it comes to the consideration of areas such as decarbonisation and job creation (see Article 30, Article 31.2.b and Article 32.2.b, EU-Angola SIFA; Article 19.3.8, EU-New Zealand FTA).

One area where there is limited domestic alignment between investment and sustainable development objective relates to gender equality. Provisions addressing investment and gender only appear in a limited number of treaties – namely, the EU-Angola SIFA, the Chile-Canada FTA, and the EU-New Zealand FTA. None of them expressly calls for investment policies to actively advance gender objectives. In fact, treaties only go as far as recognise the role that investment policies play in advancing gender equality and the importance of incorporating a gender perspective into investment relationships (see Article 35, EU-Angola SIFA; Article 19.4.1, EU-New Zealand FTA). In their stronger language, they reaffirm the parties' commitment to either adopt and implement gender equality laws and regulations – without creating any explicit link to investment and economic empowerment – or to implement the treaty itself in a manner that promotes gender equality (see Article N-01bis.6, Chile-Canada FTA; Article 35, EU-Angola SIFA). As such, the alignment between the IIA sample and FDIQR principle 2.b is overall limited.

There are several options available to states wishing to ensure increased policy coherence between investment and gender equality objectives in their IIAs. For example, they can decide to strengthen existing commitments relating to the implementation of the treaty in a manner conducive to gender equality, turning relevant provisions into either best effort obligations or obligations of result. Parties could also actively co-operate in the achievement of gender equality in the context of investment relations, for example by outlining activities for collaboration in support of women.

### *FDIQR principle 4.b: Investment promotion*

FDIQR principle 4.b recommends linking investment promotion activities to sustainable development objectives. The FDI Qualities Policy Toolkit identifies several ways in which Investment Promotion Agencies can create such linkages, including through prioritisation, policy advocacy, and the removal of information barriers preventing foreign investors' access to new opportunities.

Treaties in the IIA sample often address FDIQR principle 4.b from the perspective of prioritisation. They set out an obligation either of result or of best efforts (or, in case of the Singapore-Australia GEA, a non-binding commitment) to encourage investment in certain key sectors. In the decarbonisation area, these include sustainable production and consumption (Article 33, EU-Angola SIFA), environmental goods and services (Article 33, EU-Angola SIFA; Article 19.4, EU-New Zealand FTA), climate change mitigation and adaptation (Article 26, Investment Protocol to the AfCFTA; Article 33, EU-Angola SIFA), sustainable food systems (paragraph 9.a.xii, Singapore-Australia GEA), renewable energy and low carbon technologies (Article 26, Investment Protocol to the AfCFTA; Article 13.13, EU-New Zealand FTA), and natural resources and raw materials (Article 13.13, EU-New Zealand FTA).

In a limited number of cases, treaties in the IIA sample go a step further by providing additional guidance as to what investment promotion activities entail. For example, the Investment Protocol to the AfCFTA (Article 6) sets out a general provision on investment promotion, stating that parties shall endeavour to undertake activities such as awareness raising (e.g. organisation of joint activities between the parties' Investment Promotion Agencies, conferences and seminars, and information exchanges sessions), policy and advocacy (e.g. collaboration with regional economic communities and the Investment Agency of the AfCFTA), and provision of aftercare services (e.g. business matching activities with domestic firms). Similarly, the EU-New Zealand FTA clarifies through an interpretative provision that investment promotion will entail awareness raising and public information campaigns, the adoption of conducive policy frameworks, and the uptake of sustainability assurance schemes, especially for SMEs (Article 19.11.5). With specific reference to the energy sector, investment promotion under the EU-New Zealand FTA also entails awareness raising on environmentally friendly policies and best practices and promotion of R&D activities on energy efficiency and raw materials (Article 13.13).

The precise guidance in provisions such as those enshrined in the Investment Protocol to the AfCFTA and in the EU-New Zealand FTA may be useful to facilitate the domestic implementation of international obligations in alignment with FDIQR principle 4.b. States could evaluate whether to identify, in their IIAs, specific investment promotion activities contributing to the achievement of sustainable development objectives. For the time being, guidance is limited to the decarbonisation area, including from an innovation and R&D perspective. However, states are not limited to this area alone, having the option to consider also investment promotion activities in other areas, including gender equality.

### *FDIQR principle 4.c: Investment facilitation*

FDIQR principle 4.c addresses investment facilitation and suggests avenues on how to improve its link with sustainable investment objectives. In this sense, the FDIQR goes beyond the traditional understanding of investment facilitation to look at the broader institutional, policy and legal environment where the investment takes place, with a view to strengthening linkages with specific sustainable development-related areas such as decarbonisation, productivity and innovation, gender equality and quality jobs.

The IIA sample treaties focus investment facilitation efforts on two main areas, namely decarbonisation and productivity and innovation. The approach followed is similar to the one used for investment promotion. First, treaty provisions would identify specific areas or sectors where investment facilitation efforts should be directed. These include, among others, sustainable production and consumption (Article 33.1, EU-Angola SIFA), climate mitigation and adaptation (Article 33.1, EU-Angola SIFA; Article 26, Investment Protocol to the AfCFTA), and environmental goods and services (Article 33.1, EU-Angola SIFA; Article

19.11, EU-New Zealand FTA). Certain treaties, such as the EU-Angola SIFA, adopt a systematic approach to climate change mitigation and adaptation, by extending investment facilitation efforts to sectors with indirect relevance to the same, such as biodiversity, sustainable management of forests, and sustainable management of marine ecosystems and biological resources (Articles 33.3, 33.5 and 33.6, EU-Angola SIFA).

When it comes to investment facilitation, however, IIA sample treaties do not provide any guidance on what activities parties should implement for this purpose. The only exception is the EU-New Zealand FTA (Article 19.11). This treaty, however, considers investment facilitation jointly with investment promotion and seems to focus mostly on the latter, as relevant "investment promotion and facilitation activities" involve awareness raising, the adoption of conducive policy frameworks and the uptake of transparent, factual and non-misleading sustainability schemes. It is true that IIA sample treaties already include general provisions on investment facilitation that may apply also to investments in the decarbonisation area. However, the range of activities that parties could implement in this area is much broader and can extend to the provision of specific aftercare services aimed at identifying low-carbon business partners, organise matchmaking activities, and engage in training/advocacy activities to support the development of local workforce.

In the innovation area, IIA sample treaties seek to encourage linkages between the foreign investor and domestic SMEs, mostly through the establishment of domestic suppliers databases. The reference to this tool is particularly important, as it is considered under the FDIQR as an instrument to break down information barriers and facilitate spill overs between domestic and foreign firms. Obligations in these areas are drafted in mostly weak and general terms (Article 11, EU-Angola SIFA; Article 24, WTO IFD Agreement; Article 10.2, Chile-Singapore-New Zealand DEPA).

Despite being drafted in a non-binding manner, the relevant provision in the WTO IFD Agreement goes further than the others by providing additional guidance on the features of the domestic suppliers database. In particular, the WTO IFD Agreement (Article 24) clarifies that the database should be made available online in one of the WTO official languages, kept regularly updated and be searchable by sector or industry, company, product or service, location, certifications. Linkages are also pursued through the establishment of skills development programmes, which seek to increase the capacity of local labour force to anticipate and meet the needs of foreign investors. These initiatives are also references in the WTO IFD Agreement, which encourages parties to "to implement programmes that strengthen the capabilities of local suppliers, especially [SMEs], to meet sourcing demands of investors of other Members/Parties" (Article 25). Also in this case, the provision is drafted in a non-binding manner. Yet, it remains notable as it is the only reference to skills development programmes that appears in the IIA sample.

Further research could evaluate whether future treaties should build on current practice in the IIA sample by clarifying the links between investment facilitation and sustainable development objectives, especially in the areas of decarbonisation and innovation. In the decarbonisation area, states may rely on the FDIQR to derive additional guidance on what investment facilitation in low carbon projects entails. This could include, for example, to business-to-business initiatives in support of the green transition, such as business matchmaking initiatives or information events seeking to showcase green technologies. In the innovation area, a useful starting point could be the strengthening of obligations concerning the establishment of domestic suppliers' databases, with a view to turning them into clear and enforceable obligation of result. Additional facilitation activities could also be envisaged, including the organisation of business-to-business events or the implementation of skills development programmes contributing to sustainable development objectives in the employment area.

#### *FDIQR principle 4.d: Promotion of RBC*

FDIQR principle 4.d concerns the promotion of responsible business conduct (RBC) in the operation of the investment, including in the context of the investor's relationship with business entities, including within its broader supply chain.

Most treaties in the IIA sample are already fully aligned with this principle, requiring parties to promote the uptake of international standards on RBC (see Article 34, EU-Angola SIFA; Article 37, WTO IFD Agreement; Article G-14 bis and Article N bis-01, Chile-Canada FTA; Article 19.12, EU-New Zealand FTA; Article 13, Switzerland-Indonesia BIT). Reference is often made to international instruments such as United Nations Guiding Principles on Business and Human Rights, the United Nations Global Compact, the ILO Tripartite Declaration on Principles concerning Multinational Enterprises and Social Policy and, notably, the OECD Guidelines for Multinational Enterprises. A limited number of treaties include an express reference to the need for the investor to implement due diligence, with a view to identifying and addressing the potential adverse effects of their activities (see Article 34.1, EU-Angola SIFA; Article 37.3, WTO IFD Agreement).

States wishing to strengthen the consideration provided in IIAs to the promotion of RBC have several options at their disposal. By way of example, they could simply adopt a stronger language in relevant provisions, going beyond declaratory terms to provide for specific obligations on the parties to promote and disseminate RBC and facilitate the implementation of due diligence processes in connection with the investment. Ultimately, the way in which future IIAs could address additional sustainable investment-related elements, in alignment with FDQR principles on RBC, will depend on the outcome of current developments in international and regional fora, including at the EU level, in particular with respect to ongoing discussions on issues such as the uptake of mandatory due diligence legislation.

### *2.3.3. Areas where the IIA sample goes beyond the FDIQR principles*

The review of the IIA sample has led to the identification of additional policy tools designed to pursue sustainable development objectives and going beyond the scope of the FDIQR principles. While they might still offer suggestions on how to shape future practice, their lack of inclusion in the FDIQR principles means that their suitability to inform future IIAs must be carefully assessed.

#### *Local content and performance requirements*

A first area going beyond the scope of the FDIQR concerns local content and performance requirements. While there is no universally accepted definition of performance requirements, these are usually understood as measures designed to compel the foreign investor to implement its activities in a certain way considered beneficial for the host state, with a view to maximizing potential benefits (Genest, 2019[4]). These can consist of the promotion of capacity building of and technology transfer to local enterprises, the performance of specific levels of R&D in the country, or the achievement of a given number of local jobs.

Contrary to general standards on RBC, local content requirements have mandatory nature for the investor. For this reason, they are often perceived as an undue restriction to the free flows of FDI. Furthermore, their overall effectiveness in achieving the desires sustainable development outcomes is subject to debate. OECD studies show that, while local content requirements may help governments achieve certain short-term objectives in targeted industries (e.g. potential learning and technological spill overs, economies of scale), they undermine long-term competitiveness and may prove to be detrimental for FDI attraction and productivity growth in the long run (Stone, Messent and Flaig, 2015[5]).

These concerns have resulted in the prohibition of local content and performance requirements within certain IIAs (in the sample, see EU-New Zealand FTA) and WTO agreements, including the Agreement on Trade-Related Investment Measures, either in general or through a targeted approach that still allow for the introduction of specific PRs on local content, local employment, or technology transfer (Nikièma, 2014[6]). In the IIA sample, mention of local content appears in the Investment Protocol to the AfCFTA. This provides that state parties can introduce "measures to promote domestic development, including local content". It provides a list of examples what such measures could entail, including: (i) granting of preferential treatment to qualifying domestic enterprises; (ii) establishing linkages with local firms; (iii) enhancing productive capacity and developing local human resources and R&D; (iv) appointing nationals of the host state in manager-level and board-level positions within the investment undertaking; (v) promoting the transfer of technology, skills and know-how; and (vi) addressing economic and development disparities suffered by identifiable ethnic or cultural groups (Article 26). Such measures are all linked to the achievement of general sustainable development objectives, with explicit mention of the enhancement of innovation, productive capacities, and quality jobs in the host state. Notably, however, the Investment Protocol clarifies that relevant measures would still need to comply with protections on national treatment and most favoured nation treatment (Article 12).

The recourse to local content and performance requirements remains beyond the scope of the FDIQR principles. These explicitly recognise that, due to the risks inherent in local content requirements in terms of competitiveness and allocation of resources, states should prioritise alternative tools and measures to facilitate FDI's linkages with domestic firms.

### *Investor obligations*

Another way in which certain treaties in the IIA sample go beyond the scope of the FDIQR is through the incorporation of investor obligations. These have recently emerged in investment treaty practice as one of the tools to "correct" the inherent asymmetry affecting IIAs (Working Group on the issue of Human Rights and Transnational Corporations, 2021[7]). They also play a role in ensuring the sustainability of the investment, by requiring that the investor carry out relevant activities in such a way as to not cause damage to public interests concerning the protection of human rights, labour rights, or the environment.

Several treaties within the IIA sample include investor obligations. In some cases, these are drafted in merely declaratory terms, as it is the case for the Switzerland-Indonesia BIT (Article 14). The Brazil-Morocco CFIA (Article 13) adopts a stronger language, setting out a best effort obligation for the investor to contribute to the development of the host state, through adherence to specific standards of behaviour addressing, among others, respect for human rights, development of local capacity and human capital, anti-corruption, and non-interference in the host state's domestic affairs. Lastly, the Investment Protocol to the AfCFTA provides for a long list of investor obligations, of both best efforts and of result, covering issues such as compliance with domestic law, human rights and labour standards, environmental protection, indigenous peoples' rights, non-interference in the host state's domestic affairs, anti-corruption, contribution to the host state's development and corporate governance (Articles 32-39).

Investor obligations are seen as one of the tools available to correct the asymmetry associated with the traditional IIA system, effectively acting as counterpart for foreign investors' protections granted through the relevant treaty (UNCTAD, 2018[8]). More generally, it has also been suggested that investor obligations could help foster positive investors' conduct and contribute to improving the quality of the investment (IISD, 2018[9]).Both effects, however, remain subject to the possibility of effectively enforcing investor obligations in case of breach. However, the issue of enforcement has yet to find conclusive resolution. Theoretically, there are mechanisms (e.g. counterclaims) that could help enforce IIA-based investor obligations in investor-State dispute settlement (ISDS). For the moment, however, the issue of enforceability of treaty-based investor obligations remains merely theoretical, as ISDS tribunals have yet to address the matter. So far, when ISDS tribunals addressed breach of investor obligations, relevant legal basis was found in domestic law (e.g. *Burlington v Ecuador* and *Perenco v Ecuador*; *Aven v Costa Rica*) or international law (*Urbaser v Argentina*). The concept of investor obligations seems, in any event, to be less relevant for IIAs that do not include ISDS (such as the EU-Angola SIFA, the Brazil-Morocco CFIA, or the WTO IFD Agreement) and do not provide enforceable rights for investors.

## 2.4. Conclusions

The stocktaking analysis shows that provisions on sustainable investment included in the IIA sample address most of the FDIQR principles. Furthermore, in most cases, FDIQR principles and IIA sample provisions have a similar scope, both in terms of objectives to be achieved and specific policy instruments available for this purpose.

There are, however, areas where IIA sample provisions have a narrower scope compared to the FDIQR principles, thus offering opportunities for consideration of additional sustainable investment-related elements in an IIA context. These areas relate to the following:

- FDIQR principle 1.d: Assessment and periodic review of FDI's impacts on sustainable development.
- FDIQR principle 2.b: Domestic alignment between investment and gender objectives.
- FDIQR principle 4.a: Awareness raising on the role that stakeholders can play in supporting sustainable investment.
- FDIQR principle 4.b: Investment promotion for sustainable development.
- FDIQR principle 4.c: Investment facilitation for sustainable development.
- FDIQR principle 4.e: Consideration of sustainability factors in investment decision making.

In all these cases, a strengthening of sustainable investment considerations in sustainable investment provisions in IIA could lead to the clarification of what treaty commitments ultimately entail, providing additional guidance as to what measures could be implemented at the domestic level. For example, they could contribute to defining what "investment facilitation" and "investment promotion" entail when directed towards harnessing sustainable investment. An additional integration of sustainable investment considerations could also result in a strengthening of parties' co-operation in specific areas, especially to enhance parties' ability to comply with relevant commitments.

## References


Genest, A. (2019), *Performance Requirement Prohibitions in International Investment Law*, Brill | Nijhoff, https://doi.org/10.1163/9789004392106. [4]

IISD (2018), *Harnessing Investment for Sustainable Development: Inclusion of investor obligations and corporate accountability provisions in trade and investment agreements*, https://www.iisd.org/system/files/meterial/harnessing-investment-sustainable-development.pdf. [9]

Nikièma, S. (2014), *Performance Requirements in Investment Treaties*, IISD, https://www.iisd.org/system/files/publications/best-practices-performance-requirements-investment-treaties-en.pdf. [6]

OECD (2022), *FDI Qualities Policy Toolkit*, OECD Publishing, Paris, https://doi.org/10.1787/7ba74100-en. [3]

OECD (2018), "Towards an international framework for investment facilitation", *OECD Business and Finance Policy Papers*, No. 47, OECD Publishing, Paris, https://doi.org/10.1787/b82771dc-en. [1]

Stone, S., J. Messent and D. Flaig (2015), "Emerging Policy Issues: Localisation Barriers to Trade", *OECD Trade Policy Papers*, No. 180, OECD Publishing, Paris, https://doi.org/10.1787/5js1m6v5qd5j-en. [5]

UNCTAD (2023), *Investment Facilitation in International Investment Agreements: Trends and Policy Options*, https://unctad.org/publication/investment-facilitation-international-investment-agreements-trends-and-policy-options. [2]

UNCTAD (2018), *Reform Package for the International Investment Regime*, https://investmentpolicy.unctad.org/uploaded-files/document/UNCTAD_Reform_Package_2018.pdf. [8]

Working Group on the issue of Human Rights and Transnational Corporations (2021), *Human rights-compatible international investment agreements*, https://documents-dds-ny.un.org/doc/UNDOC/GEN/N21/208/09/PDF/N2120809.pdf?OpenElement. [7]

# 3 Domestic practices fostering sustainable investment

This chapter reviews domestic practices from selected jurisdictions that can contribute to fostering sustainable investment, in alignment with the principles of the FDI Qualities Recommendation. Section 1 describes the methodology guiding the review of domestic practices. Section 2 provides an overview of the identified practices, reflecting on how they can be considered as possible approaches to implement international investment agreements (IIAs) at the domestic level. Section 3 draws conclusions on how the identified practices can influence the drafting of future IIAs.

## 3.1. Rationale and methodology

This chapter provides an overview of domestic practices from selected jurisdictions that can contribute to sustainable investment, in alignment with the principles of the FDI Qualities Recommendation (FDIQR). Relevant jurisdictions have been chosen to ensure an adequate balance between OECD and non-OECD countries. Regional experience and practices are also considered, looking specifically at the European Union (EU), the Southern African Development Community (SADC), the East Africa Community (EAC), and the Association of Southeast Asian Nations (ASEAN). The full list of jurisdictions from which examples of domestic practices have been selected is set out under Table 3.1.

The consideration of what states are doing domestically to harness sustainable investment has direct relevance for international investment agreements (IIAs). It can provide guidance on the policy tools and instruments that states have at their disposal to domestically implement IIAs commitments, in line with the principles of the FDIQR. To some extent, the analysis of domestic practices can also offer indications as to how IIA treaty-making practice could evolve in the future, to the extent that parties wish to integrate in IIAs additional sustainable investment elements, in line with the principles of the FDIQR.

The analysis of domestic practices is not meant to be exhaustive. The purpose of this Chapter is not to carry out a comprehensive mapping of all domestic practices that may contribute to sustainable investment, but rather to provide some examples of what states are already doing to achieve this objective. To this end, the Chapter will focus on domestic practices that provide opportunities for the consideration of additional sustainable investment elements in alignment with the FDIQR principles, as identified at the conclusion of the stocktaking exercise under Chapter 2. These consist of:

- FDIQR principle 1.d: Assessment and periodic review of FDI's impacts on sustainable development.
- FDIQR principle 2.b: Domestic alignment between investment and gender objectives.
- FDIQR principle 4.a: Awareness raising on the role that stakeholders can play in supporting sustainable investment.
- FDIQR principle 4.b: Investment promotion for sustainable development.
- FDIQR principle 4.c: Investment facilitation for sustainable development.
- FDIQR principle 4.e: Consideration of sustainability factors in investment decision making.

While there might be other policy tools and practices contributing to the domestic implementation of IIA commitments, these are not included in the scope of the current overview. Additional research may contribute to providing insights into other instruments available to states in the domestic implementation of IIA commitments, in addition to those discussed in this Chapter.

The methodology adopted in the identification of domestic practices relies on desk-based analysis of both primary and secondary sources. The former category includes domestic policies, laws, and regulations contributing to sustainable investment. It also includes the review of national practices and programmes that states have implemented to achieve sustainable investment objectives. Secondary sources cover contributions from academic literature and country reviews performed by international organisations, other than the OECD (e.g. UNCTAD, World Bank Group). Specific attention is also provided to OECD publications such as (i) Investment Policy Reviews; (ii) FDI Qualities Reviews; (iii) Sustainable Investment Perspectives; and (iv) FDI-SME Linkages reviews.

Table 3.1. Overview of selected jurisdictions

| OECD members | Non-OECD members |
|---|---|
| Chile | Botswana |
| Colombia | Brazil |
| Costa Rica | Bulgaria |
| Czechia | Cambodia |
| Finland | China (People's Republic of) |
| France | Egypt |
| Greece | Fiji |
| Hungary | India |
| Iceland | Indonesia |
| Ireland | Jordan |
| Japan | Kenya |
| Korea | Lao People's Democratic Republic |
| Latvia | Madagascar |
| Luxembourg | Malaysia |
| Mexico | Morocco |
| Poland | Philippines |
| Portugal | Rwanda |
| Slovak Republic | Saudi Arabia |
| Spain | Senegal |
| Sweden | Singapore |
| Türkiye | South Africa |
| United States | Tunisia |
| | Viet Nam |

Note: List of countries considered in the review and analysis of domestic practices conducive to sustainable investment.
Source: OECD data.

## 3.2. Domestic practices contributing to sustainable investment

States have relied on different policy tools and mechanisms to harness sustainable investment, in alignment with the principles of the FDIQR. Annex E, Supporting Documents (DAF/INV(2024)26/ADD) provides a high-level list of the domestic practices identified in the current research, including indication of the jurisdictions from which the practices discussed below are drawn, as well as additional examples of domestic practices conducive to sustainable investment.

### *3.2.1. Assessment of the impacts of FDI on sustainable development*

The FDIQR and related Policy Toolkit stress the importance of assessing the impacts of major investment projects and policies on sustainable development, to identify bottlenecks in implementation. Impact assessment processes are structured, analytical and participatory approaches that allow obtaining and evaluating relevant information before making decisions concerning the implementation of investment projects or the adoption of policies, strategies and plans (OECD, 2022[1]). These processes entail the assessment of how an investment project, or a specific policy, will affect environmental, social and other sustainable development-related concerns and the identification of the steps and measures necessary to manage possible adverse impacts. Some assessments are also done after decisions are made, to determine how much foreign direct investment (FDI) has contributed to sustainable development objectives.

Assessment processes can take different forms. States are increasingly engaging in the assessment of the positive contribution and negative impacts of FDI as a whole on sustainable development, including with respect to specific sustainability areas such as productivity and innovation, employment, decarbonisation and gender equality.

Many assessments processes are focused on the environmental and social impacts of a specific project or policy. Environmental Impact Assessments (EIA) are implemented in connection with investment projects that are likely to entail significant adverse impacts on the environment. Often, the assessment under the EIA process expands beyond the consideration of environmental issues to include an analysis of the social impacts and risks arising from the project, thus entailing a full Environmental and Social Impact Assessment (ESIA). Strategic Environmental Assessments (SEA), instead, are used for the evaluation of environmental risks posed by policies, plans and programmes adopted at the national level.

#### *Domestic practices on FDI impact assessment*

States are becoming increasingly aware of the importance of both ***assessing the overall impacts of FDI on sustainable development*** and reflecting on the characteristics of the FDI that they attract. The main challenges faced by states in this context are mostly linked to the availability of comparable data on investment and the ability to meaningfully analyse them. To this end, states are increasingly relying on tools and instruments developed by international organisations such as the OECD. Among others, in 2020 the OECD supported IDA Ireland (Ireland's investment promotion agency) in assessing the impacts of FDI on national productivity and innovation (Box 3.1).

In 2022, the OECD also further updated its the FDI Qualities Indicators, as a tool to support governments in measuring overall impact and outcomes of FDI across the sustainable development goals, looking specifically at productivity and innovation, employment, decarbonisation, and gender equality (OECD, 2022[2]). The FDI Qualities Indicators provided the basis to carry out further FDI impact assessments analysis in **Chile**, **Jordan** and **Tunisia**, under the FDI Qualities Reviews process. An additional assessment is ongoing in **Egypt**. This exercise can ultimately support the identification of weaknesses and strengths of existing policy and governance frameworks, further guiding policy reform efforts at the domestic level.

#### *Domestic practices on project- and policy-level impact assessment processes.*

At the project and policy level, the implementation of EIA/ESIA and SEA is regulated at the domestic level – and, in the European Union (EU) context (Box 3.2) – at the regional level. National processes are often standardised, building on standards and best practices developed by international organisations, industry associations and foreign investors themselves. Both EIA/ESIA and SEA entail a set of pre-determined steps, which can include an initial screening to determine whether an impact assessment is required, the preparation of a report describing the impacts of the project or policy on the environment and the measures needed to address them, the implementation of consultations with affected communities, the review and approval of the project or policy by competent authorities, and monitoring over the remaining impacts (Ahmed and Sanchez-Triana, 2008[3]).

In general, ESIA and SEA laws consistently require an assessment of all direct and indirect environmental and social risks associated with the proposed project or policy. Domestic practice in certain jurisdictions may add additional conditions, calling for the evaluation of risks affecting specific areas or values. Domestic EIA/ESIA and SEA laws and regulations can sometimes provide for the ***mandatory assessment of the impacts of the proposed project or policy on climate change***. This explicit requirement is especially important. While both EIA/ESIA and SEA broadly cover project or policy impacts on the environment – which arguably also includes climate-related impacts – providing autonomous consideration to climate risk is essential to ensure that the project or policy are fully aligned with climate mitigation and adaptation objectives.

**Colombia**, **Costa Rica**, **Lao PDR**, **Viet Nam**, and the **European Union** are jurisdictions, among many others, that explicitly require the consideration of climate change impacts in EIA/ESIA and SEA processes.

### Box 3.1. Assessing the quality of FDI in Ireland

IDA Ireland requested the OECD support in assessing the contribution of FDI to the Irish economy between 2006 and 2016, looking in particular at direct and indirect effects on productivity, innovation and employment. On this basis, in 2020, the OECD published a report focused, specifically, on the analysis of the role of FDI in Ireland's trade and global value chain integration, as well as on productivity and labour market outcomes. It also analysed foreign MNE's productivity dynamics and profiled the factors driving spillovers from FDI in Ireland. The report recommended that IDA Ireland continue to diversify its investor base, focusing on attracting technology- and R&D-intensive investments in different sectors, and to encourage expansions and reinvestments by existing investors.

The report informed the drafting of IDA Ireland's new investment promotion strategy. In line with the OECD's recommendations, IDA Ireland's 2021-2024 strategy expressly set out the agency's objective to support clients in increasing their productivity, resilience, and innovative capacity, including by strengthening their employment base through training and upskilling. The strategy also provided for commitments to identify R&D opportunities across technology-intensive sectors, such as robotic process automation, AI and digitalisation.

Source: (OECD, 2020[4]; IDA Ireland, 2020[5]).

Domestic practice also includes examples of EIA/ESIA laws and regulations requiring the project proponent to describe the ***positive impacts of the project on the environment*** in its assessment report. Highlighting the positive contribution of a project to sustainable development can facilitate buy-in from communities and stakeholders (UNEP, 2002[6]). It also ensures that projects not only avoid harmful practices for the environment but also benefit process related to environmental objectives. In addition to the **European Union**, the need to consider positive impacts appears in the EIA laws of **Botswana**, **Colombia**, and **South Africa**, among others.

Certain domestic jurisdictions require that EIA/ESIA or SEA analyse not only potential alternatives but, more radically, the ***option of a no-action alternative***, assessing the environmental consequences in the absence of the proposed policy or project. The consideration of alternatives, including no-action, has two main benefits. First, the comparison allows for improvements in the design of the project or policy, providing an additional opportunity for risk minimisation and mitigation. Second, it strengthens the decision-making process, fostering a better assessment of potential risks and encouraging public authorities and project proponents to reflect on whether the proposed action is the most appropriate to achieve the desired objectives (Craik, 2008[7]). **Botswana**, **Poland**, and the **Slovak Republic** are some examples of jurisdictions that require proponents to consider no-action alternatives in their impact assessment processes.

***Monitoring and evaluation*** (M&E) is another area where domestic practices can foster alignment with the FDIQR principles. Monitoring activities are especially important to ensure that any environmental impact caused by the project or policy is promptly addressed. It also allows for adjustments in case the mitigation measures and contingency plans envisaged in the context of the EIA process are not sufficiently effective (IISD, 2024[8]). Domestic practices vary considerably in how states address ongoing monitoring of investment projects and policies. Certain jurisdictions, like **Colombia** or the **Slovak Republic**, only provide for a general obligation to implement M&E activities. Others, like **Costa Rica** or **Kenya**, also identify specific tools that public authorities may use for M&E purposes, such as audits and on-site inspections. In other cases (e.g. **Botswana, Lao PDR**), project proponents must develop a detailed monitoring and follow up plan, including identification of M&E activities to be performed, allocation of resources and personnel, and timelines for implementation.

### Box 3.2. Impact assessment of investment projects and policies, plans and programmes in the European Union

In the European Union, the EIA process is regulated under Directive 2011/92/EU as amended by Directive 2014/52/EU (EIA Directive), which sets out a harmonised regime applicable in all Member States. The Directive provides for the project developer's obligation to undertake an EIA procedure and seek authorisation prior the implementation of an investment project that is likely to have significant impacts on the environment.

Over time, the European Commission (EC) has published extensive guidance documents, to assist project developers in fulfilling their obligations under the EIA Directive. A first guidance addresses the preparation of the EIA report, providing additional details on the scope of the environmental factors to be considered in the assessment (European Commission, 2017[9]). The guidance clarifies that climate change impacts extend to both mitigation, which looks at the impacts that the project will have on climate, primarily under the profile of GHG emissions, as well as to adaptation, thus analysing the vulnerability of the project to future changes in the climate. Concerning climate change mitigation, the guidance clarifies that the EIA report must address both the direct impact of the project's construction and operations on GHG emissions, as well as indirect impacts linked to activities ancillary to the project, such as transport infrastructure and commercial development. To further assist project proponents, the EC also issued more specific guidelines on the integration of climate change and biodiversity concerns into the EIA process (European Commission, 2013[10]).

The EC's guidance also clarifies the scope of alternatives to be considered in the EIA process. The developer is required to describe the "reasonable alternatives", as well as the motivation justifying the selection of the chosen project option based on its environmental impacts. The guidance specifies that an alternative may be considered unreasonable if there are technological, budgetary, regulatory, or stakeholder-related obstacles to its implementation. Notably, the regulatory framework set out under the EIA Directive does not provide for the consideration of no-action alternative, although this requirement can be found under the national laws of specific EU Member States (e.g. Poland, Slovak Republic).

Furthermore, the EU Directive 2001/42/EC sets out the assessment of environmental impacts of policies, plans and programmes. The Directive similarly requires proponents to assess the impacts of the proposed measures on climate. Also in this case, the EC has issued specific guidance to assist policymakers in meeting the relevant obligation (European Commission, 2013[11]). The guidance jointly considers the issue of climate change impact assessment and the consideration of alternatives, clarifying that the consideration of reasonable alternatives improves the planning process by encouraging policymakers to look for better ways to meet human needs without contributing to climate change.

Source: Directive 2014/52/EU of the European Parliament and of the Council of 16 April 2014 amending Directive 2011/92/EU on the assessment of the effects of certain public and private projects on the environment; Directive 2001/42/EC of the European Parliament and of the Council of 27 June 2001 on the assessment of the effects of certain plans and programmes on the environment.

*Implications for the implementation and future development of IIAs*

When considered in the context of IIAs, domestic EIA and SEA practices offer indications on the implementation of treaty commitments. For example, Article 13.8, para 2 of the EU-New Zealand FTA provides that, for EIA processes implemented in connection with activities related to the production of energy goods and raw materials, domestic legislation should provide for the identification and assessment of "the significant effects of a project on ... (iii) ... climate". The effect of this type of provision is to ensure that domestic legislation in each treaty party provides for the assessment of climate impacts in an EIA context. In the European Union, climate impacts are already included among the elements that must be assessed. In case domestic law does not include the consideration of climate impacts, however, compliance with relevant treaty commitments would require an amendment of national legislation.

Depending on the state parties' priorities and objectives, provisions like Article 13.8 of the EU-New Zealand FTA could play a role in supporting the harmonisation of EIA and SEA legislation across jurisdictions, by providing for a common set of requirements that they would need to incorporate at the domestic level. While there appears to be already a certain degree of consistency concerning the assessment of climate risk, additional elements emerging from domestic practices – like the consideration of no action alternatives or the assessment of the project or policy's positive impacts – could be further streamlined into IIAs and contribute to align domestic practices among countries. This integration, however, would need to be carefully assessed in the context of the broader IIA, and in particular whether the IIA includes investment protection standards. There are several examples of instances where the suspension of the investment project following the implementation of an EIA process exposed the host state to liability under relevant investment protection provisions (see, among others and more recently, *Cortec Mining v Kenya*, ICSID Case No. ARB/15/29; *Rockhopper v Italy*, ICSID Case No. ARB/17/14). In this case, it is essential to ensure that treaties include the relevant clarifications (for instance, on the right to regulate for environmental purposes) so that additional EIA requirements do not expose the state to liability.

Persisting challenges in M&E continue to affect the effectiveness of EIA/ESIA and SEA regimes. The approaches adopted vary widely across jurisdictions, with some providing only for a general monitoring obligation and others intervening more directly on the matter by requiring the development of detailed M&E plans. Yet, the lack of capacity of governmental authorities at national and subnational levels – whether ministries or other dedicated environmental agencies – to monitor and audit implementation of investments and policies may ultimately hinder the effectiveness of the M&E process (OECD, 2020[12]). Building capacity at the national and subnational levels to review and monitor EIAs can, therefore, significantly improve the environmental impacts of foreign investment. It is unclear whether and to what extent IIAs could support further developments in this area.

### 3.2.2. Alignment between investment and gender equality objectives

The FDIQR and Policy Toolkit stress that, to achieve sustainable investment objectives, domestic policies addressing investment must be closely aligned with sustainable development objectives relating to gender equality. Maximising the impacts of FDI on gender equality requires coherence between policy objectives, strategies, and actions at the intersection of investment and gender. The Policy Toolkit, in particular, recognises that policies that influence the impact of FDI on gender equality pertain to different areas, from narrow investment-level documents to broader policies addressing labour markets, SMEs, entrepreneurship and human resource development.

### *Domestic practices on the integration of investment and gender equality objectives*

The methodologies for achieving policy coherence between gender equality and investment-related objectives vary considerably depending on each country's institutional and policy framework. A common approach consists of the ***integration of gender concerns into economic policies and strategies***. How such integration is achieved depends on the specific context. In certain instances, country-level policies include the promotion of gender equality and inclusive economic development among the objectives pursued through their investment policies, without specifying the actions to be undertaken for this purpose. It is the case of the National Investment Policy of **Rwanda**, which only generally states that investments should support inclusive development by promoting gender equality and creating equal opportunities for all. While the policy focuses mainly on public investments, it also recognises that the same considerations apply to private investments (Ministry of Finance and Economic Planning of Rwanda, 2023[13]). In other instances, investment and economic policies go a step further and identify the specific actions required to integrate investment and gender concerns. It is the case of **Jordan** where relevant policies identify the specific actions that might lead to increased women's economic empowerment (Box 3.3).

Integration can also occur when ***gender-related policies and strategies incorporate objectives on women's economic inclusion and access to investment opportunities***. Thus, for example, **Costa Rica**'s National Policy for Effective Equality between Women and Men clarifies that the objective of ensuring women's economic independence must be achieved by supporting the internationalisation of women-owned businesses and developing women's technical skills, in particular through trainings on science, technology, engineering and maths (STEM) for women and girls (INAMU, 2023[14]). **Egypt**'s National Strategy for the Empowerment of Egyptian Women similarly identifies a series of policies that can support women's economic empowerment, including prioritising investments in industries that can create increased job opportunities for women, establishing gender-responsive one-stop-shops, enforcing laws that protect the rights of working women, in particular with regards to working hours, maternity leave and equal wages, and applying flexible working arrangements to encourage women's participation in the workforce (Government of Egypt, 2017[15]).

In addition to streamlining gender equality across investment-related policies and objectives, governments may also implement concrete ***programmes and initiatives supporting women economic empowerment***, either as standalone initiatives or in the implementation of broader action plans. Such initiatives may entail, among others, the organisation of trainings and skills development initiatives for women-led SMEs or the development of new financing instruments that allows leveraging private sector's capital to support the delivery of trainings and capacity building initiatives for women and girls. It is the case, for example, of the Skill India Impact Bond developed by the National Skill Development Corporation of **India**, which aims to support 50 000 beneficiaries – of which 60% are women and girls – through training and access to wage employment in COVID-19 recovery sectors, including retail, apparel and logistics (National Skills Development Corporation, 2024[16]). In **Tunisia**, instead, the 'InnovAgroWoMed' programme offers entrepreneurial training programmes for women in the agri-food sector (OECD, 2023[17]).

**Box 3.3. Supporting women's economic participation in Jordan**

The promotion of women's economic participation is high on Jordan's political agenda and well reflected in the country's strategic planning documents. The national development plan, "Jordan 2025: A National Vision and Strategy", sets out the integrated economic and social framework of the country (Government of Jordan, 2020[18]). The document identifies the promotion of equal opportunities as one of its basic principles and acknowledges women employment as one of the main challenges to be addressed. It identifies sectors with high growth potential, including for women employment (e.g. health care, educational services), and sets out actions to support the achievement of the identified objectives, including: (i) facilitating access to information on job opportunities through mobile phone job search services and female job counselling programmes; (ii) supporting entrepreneurial initiatives to provide role models and examples of activities suitable for primary school aged girls; and (iii) promoting female participation in vocational and technical training and education by designating programmes that meet the labor market needs.

The ambitions of the 2025 Vision also shape Jordan's investment promotion strategy (Jordan Investment Commission, 2016[19]). While the strategy does not contain explicit references to gender equality or women's empowerment, it emphasises the importance of attracting foreign investment that creates quality jobs. The strategy identifies a list of target sectors for investment promotion, including major employers of women such as chemicals, consumer products (e.g. cosmetics), garments and health care. Companies investing in these sectors are eligible to receive incentives and other benefits, which can support gender equality and women's empowerment through the creation of job opportunities for women.

The importance of women's economic empowerment is also streamlined across the main policy documents addressing women's rights. The National Strategy for Women, prepared by the Jordanian National Commission for Women (JNCW), aims to create decent jobs for women and to promote female entrepreneurship, leadership opportunities for women, education for girls and the provision of gender-sensitive infrastructure (Jordan National Commission for Women, 2020[20]). Another important policy document is the Women's Economic Empowerment Action Plan 2019-24 developed by the Mashreq Gender Facility under the responsibility of the JNCW, which emphasises the need to strengthen the government's capacity to address challenges to women's economic participation (World Bank, 2019[21]).

Source: OECD (2022[22]), *FDI Qualities Review of Jordan: Strengthening Sustainable Investment*, OECD Publishing, Paris, https://doi.org/10.1787/736c77d2-en.

*Implications for the implementation and future development of IIAs*

Analysed through the lenses of IIAs, domestic practices on the integration between investment and gender concerns offer an indication on how it could be possible to implement treaty provisions calling for the promotion of a "gender perspective" into the parties' investment relationship. Article 35, EU-Angola SIFA, for example, states that the parties "underline their intention to implement [the treaty] in a manner that promotes and enhances gender equality". The adoption and implementation of gender policies that promote women's access to investment opportunities or investment policies that expressly consider the impacts of FDI on women would be a sign of the parties' "intention" to reconcile gender and investment objectives under the treaty. Beyond that, the adoption of such policies and the development of relevant gender-specific programmes and initiatives could represent a concrete way to implement treaty commitments of this kind.

At the same time, the adoption of such policies represents only the first step. They will also have to be implemented domestically, through the development and delivery of programmes and initiatives that effectively support women's access to FDI-related opportunities. The co-operation of treaty parties in this area, for example through the establishment of joint programmes and initiatives in support of women's economic empowerment, could advance both the implementation of commitments emerging in IIAs and the achievement of national policy objectives. Co-operation could also extend to the exchange of information among parties on gender-related initiatives undertaken in the implementation of treaty commitments, which could lead to the dissemination of best practices and lessons learned in the area.

### 3.2.3. Awareness raising on the contribution of investment on sustainable development

The FDIQR and Policy Toolkit recognise the importance of raising the awareness of the general public on the impacts of their choices, whether related to their investment decisions, their consumption habits or beyond. The goal of awareness raising is to foster behavioural changes, encouraging stakeholders to make decisions more closely aligned with sustainability objectives. The importance of such a goal relate to any area of sustainable development. This section analyses it through the lens of two specific areas: gender equality and decarbonisation.

#### *Domestic practices on awareness raising for decarbonisation*

Acting on broader societal behaviours to foster more sustainable choices is key also in the decarbonisation area. Consumers contribute to GHG emissions both directly – through energy use in their homes and burning of transportation fuels – and indirectly through their consumption choices. "Embedded" emissions along supply chains – e.g. linked to the purchase of goods and items – account for approximately 60-70% of carbon footprints in Western households (Druckman and Jackson, 2016[23]). It is not surprising that governments have implemented several initiatives aimed at raising public awareness and understanding of carbon performance.

The primary example is that of ***sustainability certifications and ecolabelling schemes*** for household appliances, which can drive consumers towards the purchase of more energy-efficient products. In turn, higher demand for energy-efficient appliances may lead towards increased investments in low carbon technologies. The adoption of such certifications and schemes is often paired with the implementation of ***information and education campaigns***, including through social media. Campaigns are often targeted towards the most different recipients, from the general public to narrower groups such as students, government institutions, industry representatives, and non-governmental organisations. Examples of such initiatives can be found, among others, in the **SADC** member states and in **Morocco** (Box 3.4).

## Box 3.4. Awareness raising on climate-efficient behaviours

### Awareness raising initiatives in the Southern Africa Development Community (SADC)

The SADC Centre for Renewable Energy and Energy Efficiency (SACREEE) is responsible for implementing the Energy Efficient Lighting and Appliances (EELA) project in Southern Africa, to raise awareness about the benefits of energy efficient technologies. Implemented over the course of five years, the EELA project involves activities on energy efficient lighting and appliances in four areas across 21 member countries. These include, among others, the organisation of public information campaigns using TV, radio, social channels and outreach events to promote the multiple benefits of switching towards energy efficient lights and appliances.

### Awareness raising initiatives in Morocco

The *Agence Marocaine pour l'Efficacité Énergétique* (AMEE) implements several communication and awareness raising initiatives on energy efficiency for the benefit of different stakeholders. These include: (i) promotional and awareness-raising events for the general public, professionals, and specialised entities operating in the energy sector; and (ii) dissemination and publishing of technical and promotional information on awareness-raising and communication. AMEE also runs a range of awareness campaigns on energy efficiency in everyday life, aimed at the general public. These campaigns include advice spots on TV and radio, games on the radio, web games and a digital presence, to raise collective awareness of the stakes and benefits of energy efficiency.

Source: OECD based on https://www.eacreee.org/project/energy-efficient-lighting-and-appliances-eela-project-southern-and-eastern-africa; https://www.amee.ma/fr/communication-et-sensibilisation.

### *Domestic practices on awareness raising for gender equality*

Traditional gender stereotypes may prevent women from accessing employment opportunities generated through FDI. Recent data shows that women represent less than 30% of employees in STEM, while at the same time making up almost half of total occupation across non-STEM sectors (World Economic Forum, 2023[24]). Women working in STEM are also heavily underrepresented in leadership roles, especially VP and C-suite positions. The STEM gender gap affects not only women's professional careers, but also girls in school, which achieve a lower graduation rate in the field compared to men (Mostafa, 2019[25]). Factors contributing to the STEM gender gap include persistent stereotypes that associate STEM professions with qualities that are perceived as traditionally more "masculine", the lack of role models and mentors, and unconscious biases in hiring, promotion, and grant funding practices (MIT, 2023[26]).

Transforming social norms becomes key to increasing women's labour force participation and maximising FDI's positive impacts on women employment, especially in high-value sectors such as STEM. States have, for example, implemented ***educational campaigns*** targeting teenage girls, with a view to sensitising them to the opportunities offered in STEM and encouraging access and involvement at the professional and higher-education level. The practice of IDA **Ireland** is one of such examples (Box 3.5). Other countries are seeking to foster positive social changes by relying on ***reward mechanisms***. **Japan**'s Gender Equality Week includes the assignation of several awards to individuals and organisations that have contributed to gender equality objectives (Gender Equality Bureau Cabinet Office, 2024[27]).

Information sharing and awareness raising on gender-related issues are sometimes considered as public policy objectives to be pursued through regulatory measures or the implementation of specific programmes. In **Ireland**, the Gender Pay Gap Information Act requires all employers with more than 250 employees – whether in the public or in the private sector – to disclose the hourly pay gap between male and female employees and to publish a report explaining the reasons for any differences in pay and the measures proposed to eliminate or reduce them (Government of Ireland, 2022[28]). By introducing a legal reporting requirement, the act can help foster positive social changes aimed at reducing gender disparities between men and women in the workforce. **Costa Rica**'s "Equality Seal Programme" seeks to close the gender gap in private and public organisations through training and awareness cycles and the development of teaching guides, to achieve a 50/50 employment between men and women (INAMU, 2023[14]).

### Box 3.5. Encouraging high school girls' access to STEM fields in Ireland

IDA Ireland supports the "I Wish" initiative, a volunteer-led programme launched in 2014 to showcase the power of STEM to teenage girls. The initiative is implemented in partnership with private sector enterprises, including multinational enterprises (MNEs) operating in Ireland, universities, educational institutes, and governmental partners. The programme includes the organisation of outreach activities, mentorship programmes, TechForGood laptop donations, twinning programmes, entrepreneurship programmes, further education programmes and showcase events.

Among others, the initiative entails the organisation of "campus weeks", in co-operation with higher education institutes in Ireland. During the course of five days, girls at the end of their high school studies have the opportunity to attend leading universities in Ireland and gain first-hand experience on the broad application of STEM. The initiative also established an "Alumnae Circle", to provide for networking and mentorship opportunities for women and girls to facilitate their professional advancement in STEM. In 2023, it also launched an Entrepreneurship programme, where teams of girls are invited to present their STEM-related business ideas to a panel of judges and benefit from the mentorship provided by private sector partners.

Source: OECD based on https://www.iwish.ie/.

#### *Implications for the implementation and future development of IIAs*

Only a few treaties with provisions related to stakeholder awareness were identified. Concerning gender, treaty commitments mostly relate to raising awareness of gender equality laws and regulations, as provided for example under Article 19.4, para 4, EU-New Zealand FTA or Article Nbis-01, para 7, Chile-Canada FTA. Activities linked to the dissemination and sensitisation on laws such as Ireland's Gender Pay Gap Information Act would contribute to the domestic implementation of such obligations. IIA provisions addressing awareness raising on decarbonisation are even more scarce. A reference only appears in paragraph 9.g.v, Singapore-Australia GEA, which refers to the need to co-operate in the establishment of partnerships with ecolabelling organisations "to help drive demand for low carbon, sustainable and resource-efficient solutions". In this case, however, awareness raising on low-carbon solutions is only a secondary effect of the co-operation between the parties.

The analysis of domestic practices may offer guidance as to how future IIAs could support awareness raising initiatives in stronger alignment with the FDIQR principles. A first approach could be to expand the scope of awareness raising activities beyond sensitisation on current laws and regulations to address stakeholders' behaviour in specific areas. Looking at gender equality, IIAs could be harnessed to promote awareness on the investment opportunities that the agreement generates for women, especially in high-value sectors with relevance for FDI (e.g. STEM). In the decarbonisation area, awareness raising could support the dissemination and uptake of ecolabelling schemes and other virtuous practices conducive to a low-carbon transition. Additional research is, however, required to determine what is the best approach that IIAs could follow to achieve these objectives effectively.

### 3.2.4. Investment promotion for sustainable development

IPAs play a fundamental role in ensuring that FDI is channelled towards sustainable development objectives in the host state, through the performance of both promotion and facilitation activities. In most countries, IPAs are major players in the implementation of four core functions (OECD, 2018[29]):

- *Image building activities*, which foster the positive image of the host country and brand it as a profitable investment destination.
- *Investment generation activities*, which consist of direct marketing techniques targeting specific industries, activities, companies and markets.
- *Investment facilitation and retention activities*, designed to assist the investor in project definition and during the establishment phase, provide additional assistance once the project is implemented and encourage expansions and reinvestments through aftercare.
- *Policy and advocacy activities*, which are instead "horizontal" in nature and whose purpose is to contribute to the creation of an enabling national investment policy framework based on investors' feedback (OECD, 2018[30]).

While the latter two functions deal with investment facilitation (see next section), the first two functions relate to investment promotion. Investment promotion is meant to attract potential investors that have not yet selected an investment destination and is composed of activities that include marketing a country or a region as an investment destination and reaching out to investors to generate leads and win new investments (OECD, 2015[31]).

#### Domestic practices on image building and investment generation activities

Investment generation is one of the most important functions of IPAs. In OECD countries alone, 87% of IPAs conduct activities falling under this category and allocate to the same almost 50% of their entire financial resources (OECD, 2018[30]). Looking at non-OECD countries, investment generation is equally important in Eurasia and in the Latin America and Pacific region, with IPAs allocating to the same 40% of their resources (OECD, 2020[32]).

A first important component of investment generation is intelligence gathering, which contributes to defining the IPA's investment priorities. IPAs may encourage priority investments through the preparation of market studies and the analysis of raw investment-related data (e.g. analysis of press articles, proprietary data, and company data). IPAs consider sustainability as one of the key elements guiding their investment generation activities. OECD IPAs are shown to prioritise investments that contribute to employment generation (SDG 10), support industrialisation and innovation (SDG 9), and ensure access to affordable and clean energy (SDG 7) (Sztajerowska and Volpe Martincus, 2021[33]). The results of intelligence gathering and prioritisation initiatives inform the implementation of other investment generation initiatives. These include, among others, the organisation of sector-specific events, such as fairs and exhibitions, not only to market the host state as a preferred investment destination, but also to connect with potential foreign investors operating in key priority sectors. Such broader events can be paired with proactive engagement initiatives, such as the organisation of one-to-one meetings with investors and of sector- or investor-specific missions.

Image building is another of the IPAs' key investment promotion functions, after investment generation. Recent surveys show that image building efforts are performed in over 80% of IPAs in OECD countries (OECD, 2018[30]), in the Latin America and Pacific region (Volpe Martincus and Sztajerowska, 2019[34]), and in Eurasia (OECD, 2020[32]). In the MENA region, the percentage of IPAs performing image building activities increases even further, with over 90% of surveyed institutions undertaking action in this area (OECD, 2019[35]). Image building activities can be performed through different tools and activities. IPAs may develop dedicated websites or publish promotional materials, such as brochures and investment guides, targeting potential foreign investors. They can also rely on innovative tools such as blog pieces, podcasts, and videos on investment-related news. Between 2022 and 2023, Invest India published a series of podcasts where its personnel and private sector partners discussed topics with relevance for foreign investors operating in **India**, issues of national security, deep tech, and technology transfer (Invest India, 2022[36]). IPAs can also build the image of the host state as an investment destination through the organisation of, or participation in, public relations (PR) events, both domestically and abroad (e.g. general business fora, exhibitions, roadshows and fairs, high-level missions involving government officials).

Image building and investment generation activities can be implemented both individually and jointly, in the context of the same initiative (Box 3.6). Domestic practice offers plenty of examples of programmes and initiatives that pursue both objectives simultaneously. IPAs organise PR events seeking to showcase the host state's potential as an investment destination in priority sectors (e.g. innovation and decarbonisation) while at the same time offering investment generation services, such as one-to-one meetings or intelligence gathering. In some instances, investment facilitation services, such as the provision of support in the establishment of the investment, and the creation of connections with local partners and government authorities, are also provided.

### *Implications for the implementation and future development of IIAs*

Existing IIA commitments on investment promotion are drafted in broad and high-level terms, only setting out the parties' obligation to promote investment in identified priority sectors or regions. For example, Article 6 of the Investment Protocol to the AfCFTA provides that state parties "shall endeavour to promote and increase awareness of Africa as the preferred investment destination" and includes a non-exhaustive examples of what investment promotion activities may entail. Such an approach is understandable, as it allows parties to select the measures and policy tools that are most adequate in consideration of the specific country-context in which they are operating. The analysis of domestic practices may be useful to highlight additional policy tools that, depending on the context, could contribute to the domestic implementation of IIA commitments on investment promotion.

The consideration of domestic practices could also influence future IIAs, in alignment with the FDIQR. Treaty parties could explore the possibility of co-operating in the implementation of joint investment promotion activities, at the same time also fulfilling their treaty obligations. More broadly, the identification of good practices and opportunities for co-operation on investment promotion across jurisdictions may have an interpretative effect and contribute to clarifying the meaning of "investment promotion activities" envisaged under the relevant IIA.

#### Box 3.6. Investment promotion initiatives for image building and sustainable investment generation

**Apex Brazil and AbvCap**, in co-operation with partner IPAs, is implementing the "Scale-Up in Brazil" programme. The initiative provides support to international startup companies from partner countries to penetrate the Brazilian market in a more efficient way, targeting specific sector with high innovation and productivity potential (e.g. IT, agri-food, clean energy, and AI). In addition to investment promotion, the initiative includes also specific investment facilitation support. Apex Brazil supports beneficiary companies in the initial phases of their investment, including by helping them setting-up business, gaining a better understanding of the local legal, fiscal, and banking systems, and advising on the branding and marketing their products or services.

In its efforts to promote investments in the local quantum ecosystem, **Business Finland** launched the Quantum Computing campaign, which seeks to attract investments and talent into the national quantum computing industry. The programme provides targeted services to companies operating in the quantum computing sector, such as the provision of targeted financial support, participation in major Finnish exhibitions, policy and advocacy support at the EU level, the organisation of workshops, webinars, and peer-to-peer learning sessions, and matchmaking initiatives with research organisations operating in the sector.

**Invest Korea** seeks to attract and promote investments in high-tech industries through, among others, the organisation of dedicated PR events, including the Invest Korea Summit. The Summit is designed to connect foreign participants with high-level government officials responsible for Korea's investment policies, including through the provision of one-on-one business partnering services. Matchmaking services are also available, with foreign investors being able to organise meetings directly with leading Korean companies in the high-tech industry.

In line with the national strategy of promoting quality FDI, the Investment Office of the Presidency of the Republic of **Türkiye** launched a new scoring mechanism, which prioritises investment projects based on five pillars: investment size, direct contributions, potential contributions, investor prestige and SDG compliance. For the last pillar, the IPA developed a survey made up of a series of simple questions on whether investors comply with specific SDGs through their investment project. Based on the results of the questionnaire, the Investment Office then categorises investment projects, with higher priority given to those that score higher on sustainability vis-à-vis the other pillars. To ensure effective prioritisation and that the investment project aligns with sustainability objectives, the scoring mechanism is used for both *ex ante* and *ex post* analysis. The agency scores the investment project before the investor makes its location decision (potential investments), once the location has been decided (attracted investments) and after the project has been established (realised investments). As such, the scoring mechanism is also used as an impact assessment tool, supporting the Investment Office's monitoring and evaluation efforts.

Source: OECD based on https://investkoreasummit.kotra.biz/fairContents.do?FAIRMENU_IDX=13817&hl=ENG; https://www.businessfinland.fi/en/for-finnish-customers/services/programs/quantum-computing; https://www.scaleupinbrazil.com/; Presentation delivered by the Investment Office of the Presidency of the Republic of Türkiye.

### 3.2.5. Investment facilitation for sustainable development

In addition to investment promotion, IPAs are one important actor in implementing investment facilitation and policy & advocacy support in the host state. Activities pertaining to investment facilitation and retention are the most heterogeneous, due to the variety of measures and tools that IPAs can use and the different objectives to which they are linked. Facilitation services are aimed at supporting project implementation by new investors, while retention (or aftercare) services assist established investors in developing and expanding their activities.

#### Domestic practices on investment facilitation and aftercare services

Facilitation services include measures such as the provision of assistance with project definition (e.g. information on local suppliers and clients, working meetings, site visits) and assistance of administrative procedures (e.g. visa procedures, work permits, tax registration, licences and approvals), as well as sometimes support in securing the necessary financing to implement the project. The analysis of domestic practice offers examples of how traditional facilitation services have been tailored to the achievement of sustainable development objectives.

IPAs – or other relevant state agency, depending on the specific host country context – can enhance the investment's contribution to sustainable development through the provision of dedicated ***sustainability advisory services***, addressing issues such as environmental protection, labour creation, innovation and gender equality. For example, LuxInnovation, the national innovation agency of **Luxembourg** fulfilling investment promotion and facilitation responsibilities, has established a dedicated Sustainability Innovation

Hub to support companies in increasing their sustainability. As part of these efforts, the "Fit 4 Sustainability" programme helps companies assessing and reducing their environmental impacts to decrease costs, improve their reputation, and gain new clients that also embrace sustainability values. The programme provides consulting services – through accredited independent consultants – to eligible companies for the preparation of environmental studies on one or more sustainability issues (e.g. carbon emissions, energy, water, life cycle analysis). Assistance also covers the development of an action plan setting out recommendations on how to meet sustainability objectives, providing guidance on how to receive financial support, and identifying measures to implement relevant recommendations (LuxInnovation, 2024[37]).

IPAs are also increasingly providing targeted support to investors with the completion of administrative procedures for the implementation of green investment projects. This can be done through the establishment of ***one-stop-shops*** dedicated to investments in specific priority sectors, in particular energy, or the establishment of "***green carpets***", seeking to fast track the approval of investment projects in areas contributing to decarbonisation. **Iceland**, **Latvia**, the **Philippines** and **South Africa** are only some examples of states that have implemented measures of this kind (Box 3.7).

As for aftercare services, these are aimed at resolving issues encountered by foreign investors in the operation of their project and supporting its expansion, including by fostering linkages with the local economy, troubleshooting issues that investors may face and providing support in the mitigation of potential conflicts, including in an ombudsman function. Concerning this latter function, **Korea** Invest has established ***foreign investment ombudsman***, which investigates and handles complaints of foreign investors and foreign-invested companies. The foreign investment ombudsman can also develop improvement measures for foreign investment system and deliver proposals to related administrative or public organisations (Invest Korea, 2024[38]).

Looking specifically at linkages initiatives, these may entail the establishment of ***domestic supplier databases***, online tools that allow foreign investors to find information on domestic companies able to provide domestically manufactured goods and services. Domestic supplier databases mostly focus only on those firms that meet certain requirements, in particular concerning sustainability performance, or operate in certain sectors. Among others, the Council for the Development of **Cambodia**, with the support of the World Economic Forum, developed a Suppliers Database with Sustainability Dimensions (SD2) to improve linkages between foreign firms and domestic suppliers. These can register their companies on the database, which highlights their sustainability characteristics across six sustainability dimensions: (i) gender and inclusion; (ii) environmental sustainability; (iii) employee capacity building; (iv) employee care; (v) responsible supply chains; and (vi) quality standards and certifications (Council for the Development of Cambodia, 2024[39]).

Linkages can also be fostered through the provision of ***matchmaking services***, and the organisation of business-to-business (B2B) meetings, connecting domestic and foreign firms. These initiatives allow representatives of foreign and domestic firms to meet and discuss potential local sourcing and business partnership opportunities (OECD, 2023[40]). The provision of matchmaking services can be targeted to investors operating in key sectors contributing to sustainable development objectives. In the **Slovak Republic**, the national IPA, SARIO, supports several matchmaking programmes targeting foreign firms and their affiliates, including the flagship "Business Link" events and the Slovak Matchmaking Fairs (OECD, 2022[41]). The latter is the largest international B2B event in the country, focusing on facilitating bilateral talks between domestic and foreign companies and the presentation of partnership offers, tenders, available production capacities, joint ventures creation demands and opportunities for co-operation. The event targets specific priority sectors, including energy, engineering industry, automotive, chemical, wood, IT, electro engineering, smart industry, and future mobility and electromobility (SARIO, 2024[42]).

Investment facilitation and aftercare services can also be paired with other types of support seeking to promote supply chain development and strengthening SMEs' absorptive capacities. One example is that of ***supplier development programmes***, initiatives designed to increase the capacity of local firms and domestic suppliers to meet the needs of foreign investors. The Suppliers Clubs programme in **Portugal** is a flagship initiative of the national IPA to integrate domestic companies into global value chains. The programme delivers a package of support services that help local SMEs collaborate with foreign investors. These include matchmaking services to assist in the identification of collaboration opportunities; business consulting and training opportunities provided by foreign investors to their suppliers; and targeted financial support to help SMEs upgrade their technological capabilities. Through this comprehensive approach to supply chain development, Portuguese SMEs can increase their opportunities of becoming partners and suppliers of foreign firms (OECD, 2022[43]).

### Box 3.7. Streamlining administrative processes for investments in the renewable energy sector

The **Investment and Development Agency of Latvia**, established under the Ministry of Economics, offers a "Green Corridor" for investments in certain priority sectors, including ICT, bioeconomy, smart materials, biomedicine, smart energy and mobility, constructions and logistics. The green corridor shortens the time for administrative procedures by half for territorial planning, residence permits and foreign workforce attraction. Investment projects are eligible for access to the green corridor if they satisfy specific requirements concerning the amount of the investment, the amount of expected exports, the creation of new jobs, and the amount of investment in R&D. Eligible investment projects must create a minimum of 50-75 new jobs with salaries in line with the monthly average for Latvia. Furthermore, eligible companies must also commit to dedicate a minimum of EUR 250.000 to R&D activities over three years.

**Business Iceland**, the national agency responsible for, among others, facilitating foreign investment in the Icelandic economy, has established a "green carpet" for sustainable investment projects, in line with the government's goal of prioritising sustainability. Investment projects that support the government's climate goals are entitled to benefit from a special one-stop-shop and facilitation support services. Business Iceland handles requests for meetings with the relevant ministries/institutions and applications on behalf of projects to become part of the "green carpet". Sustainable economic activities eligible to receive facilitation services are those that fulfil the criteria set out under the EU Taxonomy Regulation. To oversee the operationalisation of the "green carpet", the Ministry of Environment, Energy and Climate appointed a high-level co-ordinating body with representatives from key ministries and agencies, thus ensuring institutional co-ordination.

To facilitate investments in renewable energies, in 2019 the Government of the **Philippines** established a dedicated Energy Virtual One-Stop-Shop (EVOSS). This is a web-based filing and monitoring system for energy related applications, which also includes a repository of information and permits issued for energy projects. The system is shared by all entities involved in the approval process. The EVOSS promotes transparency and accountability among agencies and allows regulators and stakeholders to work together by enhancing ease of doing business in the energy sector. The EVOSS ensures the co-ordinated submission and synchronous processing of all required data and information. It also provides a single decision-making portal for actions on applications for permits or certifications related to new power generation, distribution or transmission projects.

In 2023, **InvestSA**, South Africa's IPA, launched Energy One-Stop-Shop, which offers a single point of entry for all energy projects. The one-stop-shop co-ordinates all approval procedures across the government, resulting in a streamlined and effective energy application process. The service also provides centralised information on various energy projects to facilitate new investments into South Africa's energy sector. The Energy One-Stop-Shop results in increased transparency in the energy sector, as it allows for the monitoring of progress in the approval process, better communication with developers and strengthened co-ordination among interested entities.

Source: OECD based on https://www.evoss.ph/Home/About; http://energyoss.gov.za/; https://www.invest.is/the-green-carpet; and https://investinlatvia.org/en/useful-information/why-invest/green-channel.

IPAs can also contribute to reducing labour mismatches and shortages in FDI sectors through the implementation of ***skill development programmes*** aimed at increasing the capacity of local labour force to anticipate and meet the needs of foreign investors. IPAs can become responsible for the co-ordination and funding of training opportunities for actual and prospective employees, also through the establishment of partnerships with interested private sector members. The establishment of vocational education and training (VET) programmes – which combine school-based education and on-the-job training – can help bridge the labour gap by establishing a linkage between foreign companies and highly skilled young employees (Box 3.8).

### Box 3.8. Skills development in support of the FDI labour market

The **Rwanda Development Board** (RDB), Rwanda's IPA, provides key services targeting skills development to improve the employability of Rwandans workers. To better align skills development with labour market demands, in 2018 the RDB established the Chief Skills Office. Its objectives include: (i) promoting and co-ordinating sector skills and capacity development strategies and actions to respond to the needs of the private sector; and (ii) facilitating labour market integration through strategic partnerships. The RDB works with chambers of commerce in priority sectors – and in particular tourism, ICT and manufacturing – to support member companies in addressing constraints that hamper their growths. It also establishes partnerships with companies to provide strategic investment projects with personnel with necessary skills and qualifications.

Since 1997, **AICEP**, the Portuguese IPA, has been managing INOV Contacto, an international professional internship programme that places highly qualified graduates in foreign MNEs and Portuguese firms with offices abroad for a period of 6-9 months. The programme aims to support the internationalisation of Portuguese firms through the integration of highly skilled employees in the workforce and foster links between local firms and foreign MNEs through labour mobility. The programme is structured in three distinct parts: (i) a startup one-week course on international management; (ii) a short-term internship in a Portuguese company; and (iii) a long-term internship in an MNE abroad. The programme allows young professionals to sharpen their skills in an international environment while contributing to the transfer of knowledge and skills to the Portuguese labour market.

Source: OECD based on https://rdb.rw/skills/#about; https://www.portugalglobal.pt/pt/academia-aicep/inov-contacto/.

Investment facilitation and retention services can be provided not only in a standalone form but also jointly, as part of broader initiatives attracting investments in specific economic sectors with relevance for sustainable development. The **EU**'s GET.Invest programme seeks to facilitate investments in renewable energy by linking developers and companies in Sub-Saharan Africa, the Caribbean and the Pacific with EU investors. The facility provides a wide range of services that include: (i) market and funding information, in the form of insights about countries, markets, and financing opportunities; (ii) events and matchmaking initiatives to facilitate new business contacts between operational investors and financiers; (iii) advisory support, including through targeted coaching and business advisory; and (iv) one-stop-shop services allowing energy companies to obtain information on available financing instruments, and financial investors to create visibility on the financial instruments they offer (Team Europe, 2024[44]).

#### *Domestic practices on policy & advocacy activities*

Lastly, IPAs carry out an important policy advocacy role. By gathering information on the challenges and expectations of foreign investors, they are in a unique position to deliver key feedback to governmental authorities in charge of investment policymaking, contributing to improve the investment climate in the host state. Recent OECD surveys show how almost all IPAs in OECD countries provide formal and informal feedback to the government on how to improve the investment climate (OECD, 2018[30]). Institutions in non-OECD countries are also actively considering investors' feedback in the implementation of their activities (Box 3.9).

### Box 3.9. IPA's policy and advocacy role in OECD and non-OECD countries

Every year, **Business France** sends a confidential report to the French government presenting about 20 proposals to improve the country's attractiveness. These measures result from a careful listening of foreign companies supported by the agency in their investment or expansion projects in France. The Ministry of Economy's overseas services enrich the analysis with data on attractiveness policies and key reforms carried out abroad. Proposals are prioritised by investors themselves: a panel of CEOs of foreign affiliates is jointly consulted with a private law firm to gather their views on the level of priority to be given to the various recommendations.

The **National Competitiveness Centre of Saudi Arabia** has developed a dedicated Private Sector Feedback Platform, an online tool to gather feedback on the challenges that investors face in connection with the local business environment, and in particular with the application and implementation of investment-related laws, regulations and decisions. The feedback is then channelled to the responsible government agency for the identification of potential solutions.

**ICEX-Invest in Spain** produces an annual report on the "Barometer of the Business Climate in Spain from the Perspective of Foreign Investors", based on responses from over 500 companies to a survey on their experience as foreign firms in Spain and on their future prospects. Survey responses allow the IPA to identify both strengths and weaknesses in the Spanish investment climate. The report aims to reflect the positive aspects highlighted by surveyed companies but also to stress the efforts that are needed to improve its weaknesses. ICEX also performs some firm-level analysis to understand better the characteristics and specific needs of foreign firms, depending on their sectors and countries of origin.

Source: (de Crombrugghe, 2019[45]; Saudi Arabia National Competitiveness Center, 2024[46]); OECD based on https://www.investinspain.org/content/icex-invest/en/publicaciones/barometro-clima-negocios-2023.html.

#### *Implications for the implementation and future development of IIAs*

IIA commitments on investment facilitation are drafted in similar terms to those on investment promotion and are often addressed jointly with them. For example, Article 33, para 1, EU-Angola SIFA broadly states that "the Parties shall facilitate and encourage investment in sustainable production and consumption, in environmental goods and services, and investment of relevance for climate change mitigation and adaptation". Also in this case, the provision is broad in nature and leaves flexibility to the parties on choice of tools and measures that are appropriate based on the context. The analysis of domestic practices can provide useful guidance as to what such tools and measures might be, supporting the implementation of international commitments. Similarly, domestic practices may play a role in shaping the drafting of future IIAs, both by guiding parties' co-operation in the joint implementation of treaty commitments or through their potential interpretative effect.

### *3.2.6. Promoting the consideration of ESG criteria*

Sustainable finance is generally defined as the process of considering environmental, social and governance (ESG) factors when making investment decisions, leading to increased longer-term investments into sustainable economic activities and projects (Boffo and Patalano, 2020[47]). In recent years, the consideration of ESG factors in the investment decisions has received increased attention from corporations, financial institutions, and governmental authorities alike. This is due, on the one hand, to the industry's acknowledgement that ESG investing has the potential to improve risk management and lead to returns that are not inferior to those from traditional financial investments. On the other hand, increased societal pressure, arising from environmental and social concerns including climate change, are pushing financial and non-financial investors to actively consider ESG factors in their activities.

### *Domestic practices on the development of ESG frameworks*

The push towards increased ESG considerations has led to several developments at the domestic and international level. A key one has been the proliferation, over time, of voluntary ESG frameworks, meaning principles and standards that guide investors in the disclosure of their non-financial impacts (Box 3.10). These frameworks provide valuable information on the ESG elements that should be subject to disclosure. However, several challenges hinder their effectiveness. Inconsistencies in the construction of ESG ratings across providers, the multitude of different metrics, and the insufficient quality of forward-looking metrics prevent the development of consistent and comparable information on transition risks and opportunities across firms and jurisdictions (OECD, 2023[48]).

#### Box 3.10. Examples of ESG frameworks and metrics

The **Global Reporting Initiative** (GRI), a multi-stakeholder initiative whose mission is to improve the quality, rigor, and utility of sustainability reporting, launched the GRI Standards, as the global best practice for reporting on ESG impacts. The Standards are structured as a set of interrelated modules designed to assist companies in meeting their sustainability reporting requirements. They include universal standards that apply to all organisations, sector specific-standards (e.g. energy, mining, agriculture), and topic-specific standards, addressing specific ESG issues such as biodiversity, carbon emissions, and labour rights, among others.

The **International Financial Reporting Standards** (IFRS) **Foundation** created the International Sustainability Standards Board (ISSB) in 2021, to address the fragmentation of the landscape of voluntary sustainability standards. In 2023, the ISSB developed the IFRS Sustainability Disclosure Standards as a comprehensive global baseline of sustainability reporting standards. To date, the IFRS Sustainability Disclosure Standards include two sustainability reporting standards: the General Requirements for Disclosure of Sustainability-related Financial Information (IFRS S1), which is the core framework for the disclosure of material information about sustainability-related risks; and the Climate-related Disclosures (IFRS S2), a first thematic standard setting out requirements for the disclosure of climate-related risks and opportunities.

At the thematic level, framework providers specific to climate risks used to include the **Taskforce on Climate-related Financial Disclosures** (TCFD). The related TCFD recommendations, designed to solicit decision-useful, forward-looking information related to climate impacts of investors, were structured around four thematic areas: governance, strategy, risk management, and metrics and targets. In 2023, the TCFD was disbanded and the monitoring on climate-related disclosures was transferred under the umbrella of the IFRS Foundation. The TCFD recommendations, however, remain a key ESG framework and provided the basis that the ISSB used to develop the IFRS S2 on Climate.

Source: OECD based on https://www.globalreporting.org/how-to-use-the-gri-standards/gri-standards-english-language/; https://www.ifrs.org/issued-standards/ifrs-sustainability-standards-navigator/; https://www.fsb-tcfd.org/recommendations/.

In parallel with the development of voluntary ESG frameworks, national legislators have launched initiatives to "harden" ESG requirements through the adoption of mandatory non-financial disclosure laws. These address mostly financial institutions and large listed companies, requiring them to disclose the ESG impacts linked to their operations. In the European Union, the matter was first regulated under the 2014 EU Directive on non-financial disclosure. The Directive required listed "large" companies and groups with more than 500 employees to disclose group-level information on environmental protection, human rights, social and employment issues, and anti-corruption. The European Union intervened again on the matter in December 2022, with the adoption of the Directive (EU) 2022/2464 of the European Parliament and of the Council of 14 December 2022 as regards to Corporate Sustainability Reporting (CSRD). The CSRD broadens the scope of companies subject to non-financial disclosure to include also listed SMEs and introduces a "double materiality" requirement, whereby investors will have to report not only on how sustainability issues affect their company but also on how its activities affect sustainability issues.

To further strengthen ESG reporting, in 2020 the European Union also introduced a Taxonomy Regulation establishing a framework to facilitate sustainable investment (Box 3.11). Following the EU's initiative, other countries and regional groupings have started to develop their own taxonomies. Notable is the example of the ASEAN Taxonomy on Sustainable Finance, which seeks to contribute to the harmonisation of sustainable finance practices across ASEAN countries (Box 3.12).

### Box 3.11. The EU Taxonomy Regulation on sustainable investment

The EU Taxonomy is a regulatory classification system that helps investors and companies define which economic activities are environmentally sustainable. To qualify as environmentally sustainable, the activity must substantially contribute to at least one of six environmental objectives (i.e. Climate Change Mitigation, Climate Change Adaptation, Sustainable Use and Protection of Water and Marine Resources, Transition to a Circular Economy, Pollution Prevention and Control, and the Protection and Restoration of Biodiversity and Ecosystems), while at the same time not significantly harming any of these objectives and meeting minimum social safeguards. The activities must also comply with technical screening criteria established from time to time.

The Regulation is a transparency tool that will introduce mandatory disclosure obligations on some companies and investors, requiring them to disclose their share of Taxonomy-aligned activities. Reporting under the Taxonomy will be a mandatory requirement for three key users, already subject to the application of the CSRD: (1) financial market participants and issuers offering financial products within the European Union; (2) large EU companies (with over 500 employees) and listed EU SMEs; and (3) EU and Member States when setting public measures, standards or labels for green financial products or green bonds.

The EU Taxonomy is not a mandatory list of economic activities for investors to invest in. Nor does it set mandatory requirements on environmental performance for companies or for financial products. Companies are free to choose what to invest in. Companies with products and services that are not sustainable will have to state that their investments do not consider the regulation. However, the mandatory disclosure of the proportion of Taxonomy-aligned activities will allow for the comparison of companies and investment portfolios and can guide market participants in their investment decisions.

Source: (European Union, 2020[49]).

Non-financial disclosure laws and taxonomy classifications suffer some of the shortcomings that already affect ESG frameworks and metrics. The proliferation of taxonomies, each with its own criteria and categories of classification, can create challenges for investors. The implementation of taxonomies requires a degree of data standardisation to allow for aggregation and assessment of compliance in a way that is consistent and comparable (OECD, 2020[50]). The application of ESG frameworks, non-financial disclosure laws, and taxonomies classifications may be especially difficult for smaller investors, due to the burden of having to apply different types of metrics and classification systems depending on the jurisdiction.

### Box 3.12. The ASEAN Taxonomy on Sustainable Finance

The ASEAN Taxonomy serves as a science-based, inclusive method of categorising activities based on their environmental impact in the region. The ASEAN Taxonomy has diverse potential users, including member states, regulators, banking institutions, users of capital, and rating agencies. Financial instruments may adopt similar procedures to those described in the ASEAN Green Bond Standards, and future versions of the ASEAN Taxonomy will also offer a system for classifying entities and portfolios based on an aggregation of activities.

It revolves around four main Environmental Objectives (EOs): Climate Change Mitigation, Climate Change Adaptation, Protection of Healthy Ecosystems and Biodiversity, and Resource Resilience and the Transition to a Circular Economy. To qualify under the ASEAN Taxonomy, an activity must demonstrate its contribution to at least one of these EOs and avoid any adverse effects on others. Each EO has a specific focus:

- EO1 deals with decarbonisation pathways, aligning activities with the goals of the Paris Agreement.
- EO2 aims to mitigate the negative effects of climate change and enhance resilience.
- EO3 focuses on preserving natural ecosystems, biodiversity, and sustainable resource usage.
- EO4 promotes resource resilience and the shift to a circular economy through strategies like minimising resource use and effective waste management.

Version two of the ASEAN Taxonomy, developed in November 2023, focuses on classifying activities. An activity involves the combination of resources to produce goods or services and differs from the facilities used for such activities. Technical Screening Criteria categorise activities based on their contributions to EOs using quantitative, qualitative, or nature-of-activity-based criteria.

Future versions of the ASEAN Taxonomy will expand coverage to a broader range of activities across all focus sectors identified in Version 1. Subsequent versions will incorporate qualitative process and/or practice-based criteria.

Source: ASEAN Taxonomy for Sustainable Finance, https://asean.org/wpcontent/uploads/2021/11/ASEAN-Taxonomy.pdf; ASEAN Taxonomy Version 2 for Sustainable Finance, https://asean.org/wpcontent/uploads/2021/11/ASEAN-Taxonomy.pdf.

#### *Implications for the implementation and future development of IIAs*

ESG concerns rarely appear in IIAs. When they do so, it is only in the context of new-generation treaties that follow innovative approaches to sustainable investment, rather than in the context of more traditional BITs or FTAs. Paragraph 9.c.viii, Singapore-Australia GEA, for example, broadly provides that the partners "will co-operate on mutual interests to strengthen the environmental, social and governance ecosystems in their respective countries, including data sharing and FinTech solutions, to improve decision making by businesses and investors". Provisions of such kind do not necessarily raise issues of domestic implementation in the same way of other IIA commitments. The variety in domestic practices on ESG metrics and frameworks, non-financial disclosure and taxonomy laws also makes it difficult to identify concrete avenues to influence the negotiation of future IIAs. At best, future treaties could leverage the parties' co-operation to address some of the issues that currently affect the ESG ecosystem, along the lines of what is provided under the Singapore-Australia GEA. IIAs could therefore foster the parties' co-operation for the development of uniform ESG metrics and clear, comparable, and proportionate ESG frameworks, the facilitation of ESG uptake by SMEs and the exchange of best practices in the implementation of non-financial disclosure and taxonomy regulations.

## 3.3. Conclusions

The analysis of domestic practices can provide insights on the future development and implementation of IIA commitments on sustainable investment to strengthen its alignment with FDIQR principles. The impact that they can have, however, is different depending on the type of domestic implementation and IIAs provision, and the current level of alignment between IIAs and the FDIQR.

The ways in which domestic practices can contribute to shed light on IIA implementation varies depending on the type of commitment considered. High-level, general commitments provide more flexibility to the parties to decide what type of action or initiative could be undertaken at the domestic level to implement the relevant IIA. It is the case, for example, of IIA commitments calling for the parties' co-operation in certain areas (e.g. ESG, awareness raising on decarbonisation), requiring the parties to undertake action in certain areas (e.g. investment promotion and facilitation), or asking that implementation be carried out to promote certain values (e.g. on gender equality). In all these cases, the analysis of domestic practices will have a stronger weight in the determination of what implementation entails.

The contribution of the analysis of domestic practices will be more limited in case of "narrow" IIA commitments requiring the parties to act in a specific way. It is the case, for example, of treaty commitments setting out the parties' obligations to disseminate certain gender-related laws or to adopt domestic legislation on impact assessment in accordance with specific treaty-based requirements.

In terms of alignment, in IIAs where commitments are already consistent with the principles of the FDIQR, domestic practices can offer insights on what the implementation of treaty provisions may entail in practice. They may also play an interpretative role in clarifying the scope of certain high-level, broadly drafted treaty commitments, and offer indications as to the areas where further co-operation between the parties may be pursued for the achievement of treaty objectives. It is the case, for example, of IIA provisions on EIA and SEA, in particular concerning the identification of the impacts that need to be addressed in the relevant assessment report. It is also the case of the treaty commitments calling for the alignment between investment and gender policies, as well as obligations on investment promotion and facilitation.

Where IIA provisions addressing a specific FDIQR principle are not present or where the alignment between the two is only limited, the analysis of domestic practices can offer suggestions as to additional sustainable investment elements that parties may address through their IIAs – depending, of course, on the type of IIA to be negotiated, their objectives, and priorities. It is the case, for example, of M&E activities for the assessment of impacts of FDI on sustainable investment, awareness raising activities on decarbonisation and gender equality, and consideration of ESG concerns. In all these areas, domestic practices may point at additional areas that may lead to a stronger incorporation of sustainable investment concerns in IIAs, whether through the inclusion of new treaty language or by harnessing the parties' co-operation under the framework of the treaty.

## References


Ahmed, K. and E. Sanchez-Triana (2008), *Strategic Environmental Assessment for Policies: An Instrument for Good Governance*, World Bank, https://doi.org/10.1596/978-0-8213-6762-9. [3]

Boffo, R. and R. Patalano (2020), *ESG Investing: Practices, Progress and Challenges*, https://www.oecd.org/finance/ESG-Investing-Practices-Progress-Challenges.pdf. [47]

Council for the Development of Cambodia (2024), *Supplier Database with Sustainability Dimensions*, https://sd2.cdc.gov.kh/. [39]

Craik, N. (2008), *The International Law of Environmental Impact Assessment*, Cambridge University Press, https://doi.org/10.1017/cbo9780511494611. [7]

de Crombrugghe, A. (2019), "Supporting Investment Climate Reforms through Policy Advocacy", *OECD Investment Insights*, https://www.oecd.org/daf/inv/investment-policy/Supporting-investment-climate-reforms-through-policy-advocacy.pdf. [45]

Druckman, A. and T. Jackson (2016), "Understanding Households as Drivers of Carbon Emissions", in *Taking Stock of Industrial Ecology*, Springer International Publishing, Cham, https://doi.org/10.1007/978-3-319-20571-7_9. [23]

European Commission (2017), *Guidance on the preparation of the environmental impact assessment report*, https://doi.org/10.2779/41362. [9]

European Commission (2013), *Guidance on integrating climate change and biodiversity into environmental impact assessment*, https://doi.org/10.2779/11735. [10]

European Commission (2013), *Guidance on integrating climate change and biodiversity into strategic environmental assessment*, https://doi.org/10.2779/11869. [11]

European Union (2020), *Regulation (EU) 2020/852 of the European Parliament and of the Council of 18 June 2020 on the establishment of a framework to facilitate sustainable investment and amending Regulation (EU) 2019/2088 [2020] OJ L-198/13.* [49]

Gender Equality Bureau Cabinet Office (2024), *Promotion of PR / Awareness-raising Activities through a Variety of Media, Various Training Sessions*, https://www.gender.go.jp/english_contents/pr_act/act/index.html. [27]

Government of Egypt (2017), *National Strategy for the Empowerment of Egyptian Women 2030*, https://beta.sis.gov.eg/media/413391/final-version-national-strategy-for-the-empowerment-of-egyptian-women-2030.pdf. [15]

Government of Ireland (2022), *Employment Equality Act1998 (Section20A) (Gender Pay Gap Information) Regulation 2022*, https://www.irishstatutebook.ie/eli/2022/si/264/made/en/pdf. [28]

Government of Jordan (2020), *Jordan 2025 – A National Vision and Strategy*, https://gbd.gov.jo/Uploads/Files/jordan-2025/2025-en.pdf. [18]

IDA Ireland (2020), *Driving Recovery and Sustainable Growth 2021-2024*, https://www.idaireland.com/getmedia/69a2499c-ac2b-45b7-a342-e57bfb42a2de/IDA_STRATEGY_Draft_15.pdf. [5]

IISD (2024), *EIA Essentials*, https://www.iisd.org/learning/eia/eia-essentials/. [8]

INAMU (2023), *Politica Nacional para la Igualdad Efectiva entre Mujeres y Hombres. Plan de Accion 2023-2026*, https://www.inamu.go.cr/documents/10179/401246/Plan+de+acci%C3%B3n+2023-2026+PIEG/c3780d43-23f5-4749-a23e-6fb10b8f0b76. [14]

Invest India (2022), *My New India Story Podcast Series*, https://www.investindia.gov.in/success-stories. [36]

Invest Korea (2024), *Foreign Investment Ombudsman*, https://www.investkorea.org/ik-en/cntnts/i-450/web.do. [38]

Jordan Investment Commission (2016), *Investment Promotion Strategy*. [19]

Jordan National Commission for Women (2020), *National Strategy for Women 2020-2025.* [20]

LuxInnovation (2024), *Fit 4 Sustainability*, https://www.luxinnovation.lu/innovate-in-luxembourg/fit-4-performance-programmes/fit-4-sustainability/. [37]

Ministry of Finance and Economic Planning of Rwanda (2023), *National Investment Policy*, https://www.minecofin.gov.rw/index.php?eID=dumpFile&t=f&f=70143&token=4be2a577c57eea933d379cfba3c4f67974ffd6a2. [13]

MIT (2023), *The Gender Gap in STEM: Still Gaping in 2023*, https://professionalprograms.mit.edu/blog/leadership/the-gender-gap-in-stem/#:~:text=The%20gender%20gap%20in%20STEM%20has%20been%20attributed%20to%20several,pursuing%20STEM%20education%20and%20careers. [26]

Mostafa, T. (2019), "Why don't more girls choose to pursue a science career?", *PISA in Focus*, No. 93, OECD Publishing, Paris, https://doi.org/10.1787/02bd2b68-en. [25]

National Skills Development Corporation (2024), *India Skill Impact Bond*, https://nsdcindia.org/sib. [16]

OECD (2023), "Assessing net-zero metrics for financial institutions: Supporting the monitoring of financial institutions' commitments", *OECD Business and Finance Policy Papers*, No. 37, OECD Publishing, Paris, https://doi.org/10.1787/dedcfe56-en. [48]

OECD (2023), *FDI Qualities in the Middle East and North Africa: A mapping of policies and institutions than can strengthen sustainable investment*, https://web-archive.oecd.org/2023-06-21/660050%20-FDI-Qualities-MENA.pdf. [17]

OECD (2023), *Policy Toolkit for Strengthening FDI and SME Linkages*, OECD Publishing, Paris, https://doi.org/10.1787/688bde9a-en. [40]

OECD (2022), *FDI Qualities Indicators 2022*, OECD Publishing, Paris, https://read.oecd-ilibrary.org/view/?ref=1144_1144750-u5ks4jvtnl&title=FDI-Qualities-Indicators-2022. [2]

OECD (2022), *FDI Qualities Policy Toolkit*, OECD Publishing, Paris, https://doi.org/10.1787/7ba74100-en. [1]

OECD (2022), *FDI Qualities Review of Jordan: Strengthening Sustainable Investment*, OECD Publishing, Paris, https://doi.org/10.1787/736c77d2-en. [22]

OECD (2022), *Strengthening FDI and SME Linkages in Portugal*, OECD Publishing, Paris, https://doi.org/10.1787/d718823d-en. [43]

OECD (2022), *Strengthening FDI and SME Linkages in the Slovak Republic*, OECD Publishing, Paris, https://doi.org/10.1787/972046f5-en. [41]

OECD (2020), *Developing Sustainable Finance Definitions and Taxonomies*, Green Finance and Investment, OECD Publishing, Paris, https://doi.org/10.1787/134a2dbe-en. [50]

OECD (2020), *FDI Qualities Assessment of Ireland*, OECD, Paris, https://www.oecd.org/daf/inv/investment-policy/FDI-Qualities-Assessment-of-Ireland.pdf. [4]

OECD (2020), *Investment Promotion in Eurasia: A Mapping of Investment Promotion Agencies*, OECD, Paris, https://web-archive.oecd.org/2020-09-29/565263%20-Investment-Promotion-in-Eurasia-A-Mapping-of-Investment-Promotion-Agencies-ENG.pdf. [32]

OECD (2020), *OECD Investment Policy Reviews: Myanmar 2020*, OECD Investment Policy Reviews, OECD Publishing, Paris, https://doi.org/10.1787/d7984f44-en. [12]

OECD (2019), *Mapping of Investment Promotion Agencies: Middle East and North Africa*, https://www.oecd.org/investment/Mapping-of-Investment-Promotion-Agencies-MED.pdf. [35]

OECD (2018), *Mapping of Investment Promotion Agencies in OECD Countries*, http://www.oecd.org/investment/Mapping-of-Investment-Promotion-Agencies-in-OECD-Countries.pdf. [30]

OECD (2018), "Towards an international framework for investment facilitation", *OECD Business and Finance Policy Papers*, No. 47, OECD Publishing, Paris, https://doi.org/10.1787/b82771dc-en. [29]

OECD (2015), *Policy Framework for Investment, 2015 Edition*, OECD Publishing, Paris, https://doi.org/10.1787/9789264208667-en. [31]

SARIO (2024), *Slovak Matchmaking Fair*, https://www.sario.sk/en/slovak-matchmaking-fair#:~:text=The%20Slovak%20Matchmaking%20Fair%20is,Agency%20(SARIO)%20in%20Slovakia. [42]

Saudi Arabia National Competitiveness Center (2024), *Private Sector Feedback Platform*, https://www.ncc.gov.sa/en/Visuals/Pages/default.aspx. [46]

Sztajerowska, M. and C. Volpe Martincus (2021), "Together or Apart: Investment Promotion Agencies' Prioritisation and Monitoring and Evaluation for Sustainable Investment Promotion", *OECD Investment Insights*, https://www.oecd.org/daf/inv/investment-policy/Investment-Insights-Investment-Promotion-Prioritisation-OECD.pdf. [33]

Team Europe (2024), *Get.Invest - Mobilising investment in renewable energy*, https://www.get-invest.eu/. [44]

UNEP (2002), *Environmental Impact Assessment Training Resource Manual*, https://wedocs.unep.org/20.500.11822/26503. [6]

Volpe Martincus, C. and M. Sztajerowska (2019), *How to Solve the Investment Promotion Puzzle: A Mapping of Investment Promotion Agencies in Latin America and the Caribbean and OECD Countries*, Inter-American Development Bank, https://doi.org/10.18235/0001767. [34]

World Bank (2019), *Women's Economic Empowerment Action Plan 2019-2034*, https://thedocs.worldbank.org/en/doc/379131574445136942-0280022019/Jordan-WEEAP-Jan-19-2019-en. [21]

World Economic Forum (2023), *Global Gender Gap Report 2023*, https://www3.weforum.org/docs/WEF_GGGR_2023.pdf. [24]

# 4 Facilitating the domestic implementation of new FDI Qualities-aligned international commitments on sustainable investment

International commitments on sustainable investment aligned with the FDI Qualities Recommendation can only influence sustainable investment to the extent that these commitments are implemented at the domestic level. Based on a methodological framework, the chapter provides guidance on three pillars for effective domestic implementation: institutional co-operation mechanisms envisaged under international investment agreements (IIAs), the support of international organisations in IIA implementation, and the broader role of development co-operation to facilitating domestic reform processes in alignment with IIAs commitments.

## 4.1. Developing a framework for the domestic implementation of new international commitments aligned with the FDI Qualities Recommendation

This chapter examines the topic of the domestic implementation of commitments on sustainable investment aligned with the principles of the FDI Qualities Recommendation (FDIQR), as recently included in some international investment agreements (IIAs). Implementation is the process by which policies get translated into action (Bodansky, 2010[1]). International law usually leaves states flexible to determine how to best comply with their international commitments in accordance with their own legal system. Often, implementation relies on a mix of measures, including of legislative and administrative nature, and co-ordination with different state and non-state actors, at the central and local level.

It is important to recall that IIAs can address sustainable development-related issues in different ways. A first avenue considers sustainable development in the context of traditional IIA provisions, such as expropriation or fair and equitable treatment. Another avenue – which is the focus of the current research – seeks to ensure increased alignment between treaty provisions and the principles of the FDIQR, with a view to strengthening the domestic policy climate for sustainable investment.

This last category of new FDIQR-aligned international commitments raises specific challenges in terms of domestic implementation. To address such challenges, the following sections set out a methodological framework that can support the effective implementation of such type of commitments at the domestic level.

### *4.1.1. Implementation of IIA commitments: changing context and challenges*

Traditional IIAs mainly provide a set of benefits for certain foreign investors, providing compensation for adverse unlawful action that the host state could perform in connection with the investment. Such provisions are characterised by three main features, with significant consequences for their implementation:

- *They include broad treaty commitments*, as they require the host state to either afford the investor a certain general treatment (e.g. fair and equitable treatment) or to refrain from harming general investors rights associated with the investment (e.g. non-discrimination, expropriation).
- *They give rise to benefits for a specific category of beneficiaries.* Even when included in a multilateral treaty, the benefits envisaged under the applicable IIA are owed by the host state only to investors from the home state.
- *They rely on a unique enforcement approach*. If substantive protections are breached, the investor can seek compensation through the specific adjudicatory mechanism associated with IIAs, including through investor-state dispute settlement (ISDS).

Traditional IIAs have been subject to increasing criticism, due, among other things, to concerns associated with ISDS and the asymmetry between host states and investors' rights and obligations (Gordon and Pohl, 2015[2]). An analysis of the critiques associated with the IIA and ISDS regime is beyond the scope of the current research. The comparison with the traditional "protection-based" structure of IIAs, however, is useful to illustrate the specific characteristic and challenges associated with new FDIQR-aligned commitments on sustainable investment, which rest on different features:

- *They include "targeted" treaty commitments*. The FDIQR-aligned commitments on sustainable development specifically call on the host state to adopt a wide range of measures that can harness sustainable investment by improving the domestic investment climate (e.g. establish inter-agency co-operation mechanisms, undertake impact assessment processes, adopt investment promotion and facilitation measures).

- *They give rise to benefits that are not limited to a specific category of beneficiaries*. While they can be included in a bilateral IIA, the benefits that they may entail in terms of improvements in the host state's investment climate may ultimately create positive effects for all foreign investors, regardless of whether their home state is a party to the underlying IIA, as well as for domestic investors.
- *They rely on a compliance approach*. Because of the widespread benefits they can produce, the most appropriate remedy in case of breach of new FDIQR-aligned commitments on sustainable investment is not compensation, but rather ensuring that the host state adopts the required measure. This shifts the focus from sanctioning potential non-compliance to ensuring that treaty commitments are properly implemented in the first place.

The starting point is the consideration that parties bear the primary responsibility for the domestic implementation of their new FDIQR-aligned international commitments. To this end, they may rely on a wide range of co-ordination measures and mechanisms to further guide their implementation efforts. Instruments such as the performance of self-assessments, the establishment of co-ordination mechanisms, and the definition of domestic strategies and policies can all support states in identifying suitable implementation measures in line with their domestic legislative and administrative systems. These are all particularly suitable to implement FDIQR-aligned international commitments, as evidenced in recent examples linked to domestic practices for the implementation of the WTO Investment Facilitation for Development (IFD) Agreement or the Investment Protocol to the African Continental Free Trade Agreement (AfCFTA) (Box 4.1).

By themselves, however, domestic measures and efforts may not be enough. Challenges arise, in particular, for developing countries and least developed countries (LDCs) which may be ultimately unable to comply with their FDIQR-aligned international commitments due to lack of capacity or financial resources. In this situation and given the different premises on which the new FDIQR-aligned international commitments on sustainable investment rest, the need arises to develop a dedicated methodological framework seeking to facilitate their domestic implementation.

### *4.1.2. Developing a dedicated methodological framework for the domestic implementation of new FDIQR-aligned commitments on sustainable investment*

While the challenges in implementing FDIQR-aligned IIA commitments on sustainable investment are well noted, the development of potential solutions has received little attention so far. There are, however, other areas of international law where the topic of the domestic implementation of international commitments has emerged. Among others, international environmental law provides examples of obligations that share several features with IIA commitments on sustainable investment. Notably, some international environmental law instruments provide for positive commitments requiring states to adopt all necessary measures to prevent environmental damage. Such commitments do not necessarily look at specific categories of beneficiaries, creating positive consequences for multiple beneficiaries affected by global or transboundary environmental issues. Because of the specific goods and values that they protect, focus is placed on facilitating compliance, rather than sanctioning non-compliance.

Several commentators have examined the question of compliance with international environmental commitments (Dupuy and Viñuales, 2018[3]). Through their analysis, they have contributed to the identification of three main tools that can support effective implementation. First, reporting and monitoring mechanisms can facilitate information sharing and the identification of best practices. They allow states to provide information on the measures that they have adopted to implement their treaty commitments and to reflect on the suitability of the policy tools on which they have relied. Second, the provision of technical assistance, including in the form of capacity building, can empower states by providing them with the skills and knowledge required to implement their treaty commitments in an effective manner. Lastly, financial assistance can further support implementation by providing states with the necessary resources.

## Box 4.1. Domestic initiatives supporting implementation of international commitments

### Ecuador's self-assessment for the implementation of the WTO IFD Agreement

To support the implementation of WTO IFD Agreement commitments, the WTO Secretariat developed a standardised self-assessment guide to support members in determining the extent to which their domestic legal and policy frameworks are already aligned with treaty commitments. Several IFD Agreement members have already started implementing self-assessments at the domestic level.

Between June and October 2023, Ecuador conducted its IFD self-assessment identifying both the degree to which it was already complying with commitments under the IFD Agreement and areas where further action was instead necessary (e.g. on the simplification of administrative procedures related to investment). The results were consolidated into a national draft needs assessment that was then validated by representatives of different government institutions with competence on investment matters. The validated needs assessment will serve to guide domestic efforts to implement WTO IFD commitments, identifying areas where additional technical assistance and capacity building are needed.

Ecuador is not the only country resorting to self-assessment to facilitate the implementation of the WTO IFD Agreement domestically. Members of the Organization of Eastern Caribbean States (OECS) as well as the Lao People's Democratic Republic have also engaged in similar exercises.

### The role of National Implementation Committees (NIC) in supporting AfCFTA implementation

In the 2018 Assembly of the Heads of States and Government of the African Union, state parties to the AfCFTA committed to the establishment of national committees to support the meaningful implementation of AfCFTA provisions. Since then, several African countries have set up national implementation committees (NICs), including Côte d'Ivoire, Ghana, Kenya, Nigeria and Rwanda. NICs perform a wide range of crucial functions, that include, depending on the context: (i) developing plans and strategies for AfCFTA implementation; (ii) advise and lobby government around policy reform necessary for proper implementation of AfCFTA commitments and domestic incorporation of AfCFTA legal instruments; (iii) report on, monitor and evaluate policies and projects to support AfCFTA implementation; and (iv) ensure effective stakeholder co-ordination, including between governmental entities, private sector, civil society, and the donor community. Provided with these functions, NICs may prove effective in guiding domestic efforts for the implementation of the Investment Protocol to the AfCFTA and related FDIQR-aligned international commitments.

Source: (International Trade Center and World Economic Forum, 2024[4]; World Trade Organization, 2023[5]; IISD, 2024[6]; ODI, 2023[7]).

Applied to the implementation of international commitments to facilitate sustainable investment, these three tools may be used by different actors at different stages of the process leading to the adoption and implementation of the underlying IIA. It is possible to identify three different, but complementary, implementation mechanisms:

1. **Treaty-based mechanisms**: IIAs often establish institutional co-operation mechanisms composed of representatives of the parties, with the mandate to address any matter that may arise in the implementation of the agreement. In certain cases, such mechanisms can be provided with specific powers linked to information sharing and facilitating the provision of technical and financial support. State parties to the IIA can rely on such mechanisms in their implementation efforts once the IIA is in place.
2. **Support from international organisations**: Following the conclusion of the relevant IIA, international organisations can support state parties in their efforts to comply with their treaty

commitments. International organisations can provide dedicated technical assistance, harnessing sophisticated tools and processes that they have developed to identify potential gaps in implementation and guide domestic reform efforts. They can also foster the sharing of best practices in implementation, thus allowing for the identification of the policy tools and approaches that best allow achieving the objectives of the underlying IIA.

3. **Development co-operation and international partnerships**: Even prior to the negotiation of an IIA, states may rely on development co-operation and mobilise support for strategic partnerships aimed at improving their overall investment climate. Such partnerships can support information exchange efforts, as well as the performance, in co-operation with international organisations, of technical assistance and capacity building programmes contributing to the effective implementation of commitments arising out of existing or future IIAs.

The interaction among the three identified mechanisms can support the development of a methodological framework guiding domestic implementation of international commitments to facilitate sustainable investment, supporting domestic implementation initiatives undertaken at the domestic level. Figure 4.1 illustrates the different implementation mechanisms, the tools they can harness, and the phase of IIA implementation during which they can be used.

### Figure 4.1. Framework for the domestic implementation of international commitments on sustainable investment

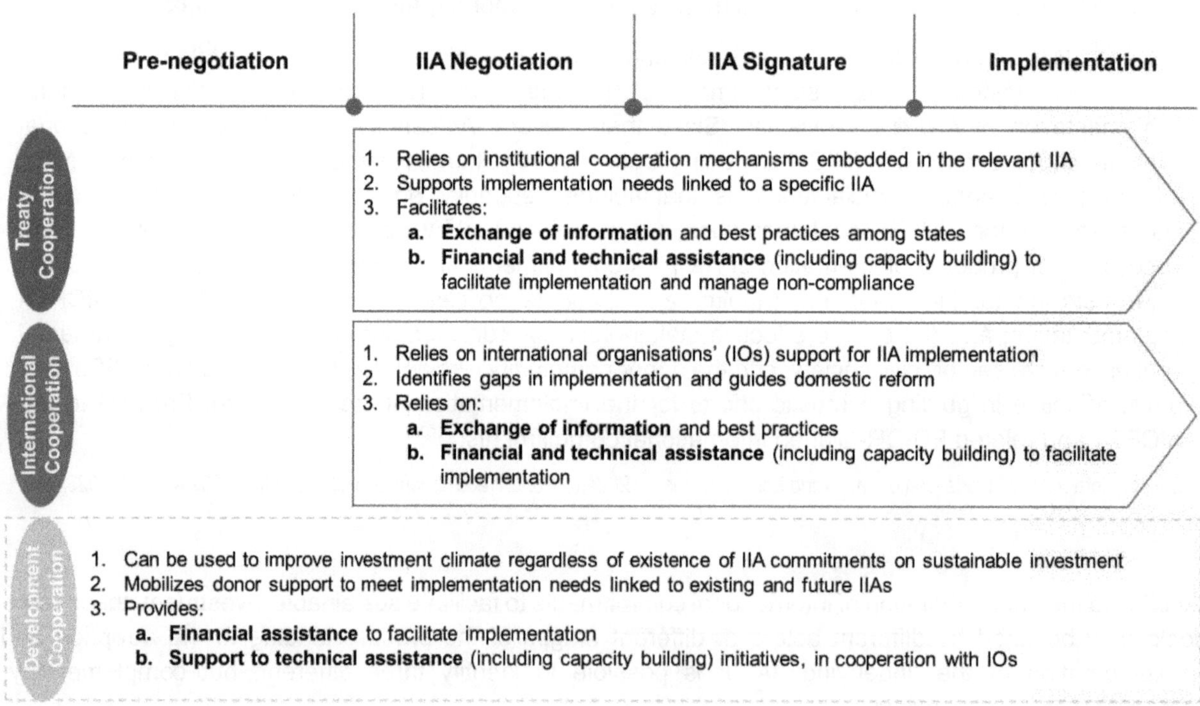


Source: OECD.

The sections below provide an overview on how each mechanism is addressed in the context of the IIA sample. Future research could also contribute to identifying and analysing concrete examples of how such mechanisms have been used in practice and the extent to which they have contributed to effective treaty implementation.

## 4.2. Facilitating implementation through treaty-based mechanisms

IIAs often provide for the establishment of mechanisms with powers to facilitate implementation. The functioning of such bodies, including the specific tools and functions entrusted to them, largely depends on the state parties' arrangement, as set out in the underlying IIA. This section examines treaty-based mechanisms established in a sample of nine IIAs (IIA sample), already subject to the stocktaking exercise carried out in Chapter 2.

With one exception, all the treaties in the IIA sample set up implementation mechanisms (Figure 4.2), often in the form of joint committees or – in one instance – joint implementation teams (Singapore-Australia GEA, Annex 1, para 15). More complex agreements, such as free trade agreements (FTAs), often establish multiple implementation bodies, each with oversight over specific areas or topics. The EU-New Zealand FTA first sets up a Trade Committee, as the main body tasked with oversight on achieving the agreement's objectives. It also creates specialised committees with a mandate over the implementation of specific chapters, including, among others, a Committee on Trade and Sustainable Development (Article 24.4, para 1). Similarly, the Chile-Canada FTA establishes a specialised Trade and Gender Committee guiding the implementation of its Gender Chapter (Article Nbis-04).

The institutional arrangements under the Investment Protocol to the AfCFTA are particularly noteworthy. The Protocol first provides for the establishment of a Committee on Investment to facilitate implementation (Article 41). At the same time, it also sets up a Pan-African Trade and Investment Agency (the Agency) with the mandate to "assist State parties, their investment promotion agencies, and their private sector through mobilising financial resources, fostering business development, and providing technical and other support for the promotion and facilitation of investment". The Agency is also tasked with supporting states in "building their capacity in the formulation and implementation of investment policies" as well as "facilitating co-ordination, interaction and dialogue" among relevant national stakeholders involved in the investment process (Article 42, paras 3-4). By doing so, the Agency becomes the main body for the effective implementation of the AfCFTA Investment Protocol.

Most IIAs within the sample provide for the establishment of national focal points or contact points. These bodies are essentially aimed at facilitating the exchange of information between the parties (e.g. Chile-Singapore-New Zealand DEPA, Article 12.6) or at providing investment-related information to investors of one party (e.g. Brazil-Morocco CFIA, Article 15; EU-Angola SIFA, Article 22; WTO IFD Agreement, Article 22). Such information exchange can also contribute to facilitating implementation.

### Figure 4.2. Institutional co-operation mechanisms within the IIA sample

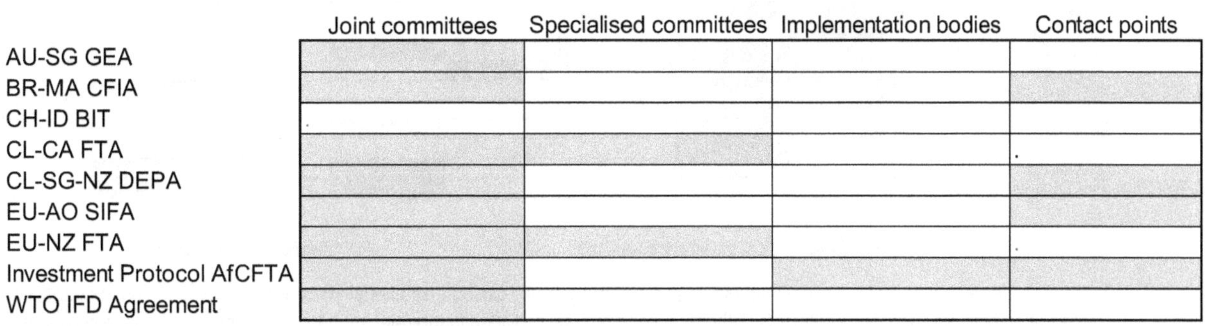


Note: This figure maps the different types of institutional co-operation mechanisms established by the nine IIAs included in the IIA sample. It shows that joint committees are the most common institutional co-operation mechanism envisaged in the IIA sample.
Source: OECD, based on the review of the IIA sample.

### *4.2.1. Composition of institutional co-operation mechanisms*

The FDIQR principles recognise that an increased engagement with stakeholders, including private sector, trade unions and civil society organisations (CSOs), is essential to enhance the impact of investment on sustainable development (OECD, 2022[8]). The same considerations apply when analysing the implementation of IIA commitments on sustainable investment, due to the broader impacts they may have on society as a whole.

Institutional co-operation mechanisms under the IIA sample are mostly composed of representatives of the parties. In limited cases, however, additional arrangements are put in place to ensure the involvement of non-party stakeholders in the implementation process. The EU-New Zealand FTA provides that each party must designate a domestic advisory group, which will provide advice on implementation-related issues (Article 26.6, para 1). The group must include a "balanced representation" of independent civil society members, business and employers' organisations, and trade unions operating in areas of relevance for the FTA. The EU-Angola SIFA provides for the organisation of a civil society dialogue for the purpose of discussing implementation. The dialogue must also involve a balanced representation of civil society members, business organisations and trade unions (Article 46). Even in the absence of specific multi-stakeholder arrangements, however, the integration of broader civil society organisations, business and employees' concerns in the implementation process may be ensured through committees' power to consult with CSOs and private sector members on specific questions submitted for discussion (e.g. Brazil-Morocco CFIA, Article 14.4, letter d).

### *4.2.2. Main functions of institutional co-operation mechanisms*

The mechanisms established under treaties within the IIA sample include a set of functions relevant for domestic implementation (Figure 4.3): They are provided with general implementation oversight functions and tasked with facilitating the implementation of the underlying IIAs. In certain instances, facilitation can occur through reliance on specific tools and mechanism such as reporting and technical and financial assistance. They can also perform functions associated with the management of potential non-compliance with treaty provisions. Depending on the underlying treaty, all these functions can be regulated with different degrees of specificity.

Figure 4.3. Overview of the functions of treaty-based institutional co-operation mechanisms

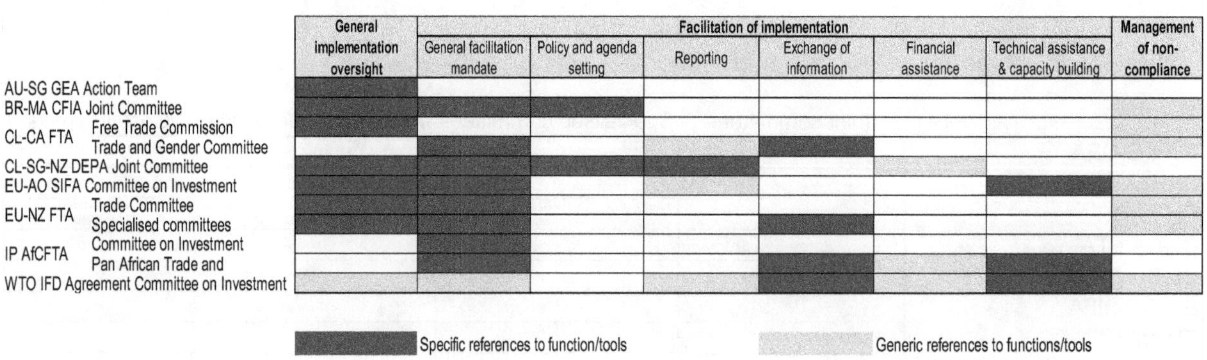


Note: This figure provides an overview of the main functions performed by treaty-based institutional co-operation mechanisms in connection with the implementation of international commitments. Other functions may be provided in the relevant IIA but are not specifically considered in this analysis.
Source: OECD, based on the review of the IIA sample.

### *General oversight and facilitation of implementation functions*

Institutional co-operation mechanisms within the IIA sample are all provided with general supervisory powers over the implementation of the underlying agreement (e.g. Chile-Singapore-New Zealand DEPA, Article 12.2; Singapore-Australia GEA, Annex 1, para 15; Brazil-Morocco CFIA, letter (c); EU-Angola SIFA, Article 44.1, letter (b); EU-New Zealand FTA Article 24.2, para 1, letter (b); Chile-Canada FTA, Article N-01). There are, however, two exceptions. First, the Agency established under the Investment Protocol to the AfCFTA does not have oversight powers, but only facilitation ones. As for the Committee on Investment under the same Investment Protocol, its specific powers will be decided by the Council of Ministers to the AfCFTA at a later stage (Article 41, para 2). The WTO IFD Agreement, instead, provides that the Committee on Investment Facilitation "shall review the operation and implementation of this Agreement four years from its entry into force, and periodically thereafter" (Article 39.7). Compared to other IIAs, therefore, the oversight functions of the WTO IFD Agreement Committee are time-bound and subject to more narrow boundaries.

In addition to oversight functions, most institutional co-operation mechanisms under the IIA sample also exercise general facilitation functions (e.g. Chile-Singapore-New Zealand DEPA, Article 12.2; Brazil-Morocco CFIA, Article 14.4, letter (c); EU-Angola SIFA, Article 44.1, letter (b); EU-New Zealand FTA Article 24.2, para 1, letter (b)). While the Committee on Investment Facilitation under the WTO IFD Agreement is not expressly assigned general facilitation functions, the specific powers and tools it can exercise essentially allow it to perform a facilitation role as well. Looking at the Chile-Canada FTA framework, the Free Trade Commission is also not provided with explicit facilitation functions, which are instead delegated to the specialised committees. Thus, the Trade and Gender Committee is expressly tasked with determining, organising and facilitating the co-operation activities identified under the Trade and Gender Chapter to align trade, investment and gender objectives (Article Nbis04, para 2).

### *Facilitating implementation through agenda setting, reporting and information sharing*

In addition to general oversight and facilitation functions, IIAs can also provide for specific facilitation-related tools and instruments. At a higher level, facilitation of implementation can be pursued through activities of ***policy and agenda setting***, with the parties jointly agreeing on avenues, activities and programmes that can help achieve the objectives of the underlying treaty (e.g. Chile-Singapore-New Zealand DEPA, Article 12; Brazil-Morocco CFIA, Article 21).

***Reporting requirements*** are also recognised as one of the main tools that can support the implementation of international commitments. They require states to share with the relevant institutional co-operation mechanism information on the measures that they have adopted in the implementation of their international commitments. By doing so, they can support monitoring efforts and allow for the identification of potential implementation gaps or challenges. A specific reporting requirement in the IIA sample only appears in the Chile-Singapore-New Zealand DEPA, with other treaties opting for a more general approach (Table 4.1). A notable provision is set out in the WTO IFD Agreement. This requires the Committee on Investment Facilitation to prepare an annual report on investment facilitation measures taken to implement the agreement, "based, *inter alia*, on information notified by Member/Parties or otherwise authorised by them" (Article 39.5). This provision effectively requires states to share information on implementation with the Committee, without amounting to a proper reporting obligation.

Table 4.1. Reporting requirements in institutional co-operation mechanisms under the IIA sample

| Treaty | Article | Reporting requirement |
|---|---|---|
| Chile-Singapore-New Zealand DEPA | Article 12.5, para 3 | At each meeting of the Joint Committee, each Party shall report on its plans for, and progress towards the implementation of the agreement. |
| Chile-Canada FTA | Article N*bis* 04, para 9 | Each party shall develop mechanisms to report publicly on the activities carried out under the Trade and Gender Chapter. |
| EU-Angola SIFA | Article 46, para 4 | The parties are expected to provide information on the implementation of the agreement only in the context of the civil society dialogue. |
| WTO IFD Agreement | Article 26 | Member states are generally encouraged to provide information to the Committee on Investment Facilitation on cross-border activities of co-operation on investment facilitation |
| WTO IFD Agreement | Article 39.5 | The Committee on Investment Facilitation shall prepare an annual report on investment facilitation measures based, *inter alia*, on information notified by Member/Parties. |

Source: OECD, based on the review of the IIA sample.

***Information exchange requirements*** seek to foster the sharing of experiences and best practices among state parties, contributing to the identification of the most appropriate tools, measures, and practices for implementation. Such requirements are only envisaged in a small number of IIA sample treaties (Table 4.2).

Table 4.2. Information exchange requirements in institutional co-operation mechanisms under the IIA sample

| Treaty | Article | Information exchange requirement |
|---|---|---|
| Investment Protocol AfCFTA | Article 42, para 4 | The Pan African Trade and Investment Agency shall facilitate dialogue between and among national focal points, investment promotion agencies and other relevant stakeholders to enable the sharing of information with respect to trade, export promotion, investment opportunities, peer learning and good practices. |
| Chile-Canada FTA | Article Nbis-04, para 2, letters (c) and (d) | The Trade and Gender Committee shall facilitate the exchange of information on experiences relating to the establishment and implementation of programmes and policies addressing gender concerns, as well as on experiences and lessons learned in the implementation of the co-operation activities. |
| EU-New Zealand FTA | Article 24.4, para 6, letter (e) | The specialised committees act as a forum to exchange information, discuss best practices, and share implementation experiences. |
| WTO IFD Agreement | Article 39.4 | The Committee on Investment Facilitation shall develop procedures for the sharing of information and experiences on investment facilitation, as well as the identification of best practices. |

Source: OECD, based on the review of the IIA sample.

### *Facilitating implementation through financial assistance, technical assistance, and capacity building*

Financial support and technical assistance, including in the form of capacity building, are key tools to support state parties' implementation efforts. Institutional co-operation mechanisms under the IIA sample do not directly provide for this kind of support, which is mostly entrusted to development co-operation initiatives and to international organisations, but they do play a monitoring role over how such support is provided to state parties.

References to ***financial assistance*** are scarce in the IIA sample. This finds only a brief mention in the Chile-Singapore-New Zealand DEPA, where states commit themselves to "providing, within the limits of their own capacities and through their own channels, the appropriate resources, including financial resources" for the implementation of the agreement (Article 12.5). Mobilising financial assistance is also one of the many tasks of the Agency established under the Investment Protocol to the AfCFTA, which "shall assist State Parties ... through mobilising financial resources" to support initiatives for investment promotion and facilitation (Article 42, para 3). Lastly, the WTO IFD Agreement envisages the possibility to establish an Investment Facilitation Facility to assist parties that are either developing or least developed countries (LDCs) in implementing the treaty's provisions. It is not clear, however, if such a Facility would be able to support beneficiary states through financial assistance.

***Technical assistance and capacity building*** receive more specific attention. The Investment Protocol to the AfCFTA explicitly recognises the role of the Agency in providing technical and other support for promotion and facilitation activities in state parties (Article 42, para 3). The obligation remains at a quite high-level, as the specific modalities for support and co-operation are not defined in the treaty itself. The Investment Protocol also sets out an obligation for state parties to support the provision of technical assistance and capacity building, in co-operation with the Agency, the AfCFTA Secretariat and existing Regional Economic Communities (Article 43). The technical assistance and capacity building initiatives considered under this provision are those made available in the context of development co-operation efforts.

The EU-Angola SIFA also addresses technical assistance and capacity building initiatives implemented in a broader development co-operation context, while also envisaging a specific role for the Committee on Investment Facilitation in this area. The Committee is identified as the forum where parties can exchange information and review progress on the technical assistance and capacity building initiatives provided in the implementation of the agreement and, more importantly, identify the needs that should guide the identification of relevant initiatives (Article 42, para 4). A similar role is entrusted to the Committee on Investment Facilitation under the WTO IFD Agreement. The treaty first recognises that technical assistance and capacity building should be provided to support developing countries and LDCs in their implementation efforts (Article 27, para 2). At the same time, the Committee represents the forum for state parties to review progress in the provision of support, to identify instances where such support is not adequate, and to share experiences and information on ongoing assistance, including success stories and lessons learned (Article 35.4, letters (b) and (c)). On this basis, beneficiary and donor countries alike are required to submit to the Committee information on technical assistance and capacity building initiatives undertaken to support treaty implementation (Article 36.3 and Article 36.4).

#### *Managing instances of non-compliance*

Treaty-based co-operation mechanisms can also contribute to managing instances of potential non-compliance with the commitments under the treaty. Such a function is grounded in the consideration that, in certain cases, lack of compliance might be due not to an unwillingness to comply, but rather to an inability to do so, either for lack of capacity or resources. In this situation, the provision of financial or technical assistance might support the state in returning into a state of compliance with the underlying commitment (Bodansky, 2010[1]). The management of non-compliance function is not specifically envisaged in IIA sample treaties, but the broader functions with which institutional co-operation mechanisms are entrusted can indirectly contribute to this objective. In general, treaties within the IIA sample grant to such mechanisms the power to intervene to solve potential issues arising from, or any matter related to, implementation, which could be interpretatively understood to include management of instances of non-compliance (e.g. Brazil-Morocco CFIA, Article 19, para 1 letter (e); EU-New Zealand FTA, Article 19.15, para 2, letter (c) and Article 24.4, para 6, letter (b); Chile-Canada FTA, Article N-01, para 2, letter (c)).

The Committee on Investment Facilitation under the EU-Angola SIFA includes among its functions that of seeking "ways and methods of preventing or solving problems that may arise in areas covered by the agreement" (Article 44, para 1). This problem-solving function could be well understood as referring to the resolution of instances of non-compliance with treaty commitments. In this context, the Committee may also be able to rely on its power to issue recommendations (Article 45, para 2). It could be possible for the Committee to recommend a specific course of action to deal with the potential non-compliance, such as the identification of technical assistance and capacity building initiatives to support the non-complying party. The WTO IFD Agreement similarly encourages the parties to raise before the Committee on Investment Facilitation any questions relating to issues on the implementation and application of the treaty (Article 39.8) and recognises the key role that the Committee plays in facilitating the prompt development of "mutually satisfactory solutions" (Article 39.9). The WTO IFD Agreement is also notable in that it seeks to prevent potential non-compliance by member parties by providing for a differential implementation regime for developing countries and LDCs (Box 4.2). Notably, it explicitly links implementation with necessary capacity and resources, with the consequence that a country lacking capacity will not be required to implement relevant treaty provisions until that capacity has been acquired.

### *4.2.3. Implications for domestic implementation*

Institutional co-operation mechanisms offer a first avenue for the parties to support the domestic implementation of new FDIQR-aligned commitments on sustainable investment. By harnessing policy and agenda-setting functions, treaty-based mechanisms can support the identification of measures and actions that the parties could consider adopting in the implementation of IIA commitments. They could also perform a monitoring function over implementation, identifying challenges and bottlenecks and recommending potential avenues to address them. Furthermore, they could promote the development of synergies with international organisations and facilitate development co-operation linkages, also with a view to obtaining support for domestic implementation of treaty commitments on sustainable investment.

The possibility for institutional co-operation mechanisms to perform such role, however, rests on a series of key conditions. In particular, it is not sufficient for the IIA to provide for the establishment of such a mechanism, but it needs to be sufficiently anchored within domestic strategies and administrations over the long term. Parties must involve the relevant administrations and follow up on implementation at central and local levels. Parties must also have the political will to use it, as well as ensure that the mechanism is properly funded. Also in this case, the role of development co-operation in supporting institutional co-operation mechanisms could be further explored.

#### Box 4.2. Special and differential treatment in the WTO IFD Agreement

The WTO IFD Agreement includes special and differential treatment (SDT) provisions (Section V of the Agreement) seeking to facilitate developing countries and LDCs in their efforts to implement treaty commitments. Developing countries and LDCs are expected to implement the commitments of the WTO IFD Agreement only when they have acquired the necessary capacity to do so. Until then, they can benefit from more flexible deadlines and receive technical assistance and support for capacity building, with a view to strengthening their implementation abilities.

Developing countries and LDCs can classify their commitments into three categories based on a self-designation process. For each category, different implementation timeframes apply, with Category B commitments being subject to a transitional period where no implementation is required and Category C commitments being subject to the provision of assistance and capacity building support. States facing difficulties in meeting implementation deadlines can request extensions. To this end, they must inform the Committee on Investment Facilitation of the new dates for implementation and provide a justification for the delay, specifying the need for further assistance, the existence of unforeseen circumstances, and obstacles in finding support.

In case of unforeseen circumstances that prevent implementation or when an extension of implementation deadline is not possible, states can rely on the support provided by a group of independent experts, which will issue recommendations proposing the actions that the Committee may adopt to assist members in complying.

Source: WTO IFD Agreement, Articles 27 ff.

## 4.3. International co-operation to align domestic reforms and international commitments

State parties to an existing IIA can request the support of international organisations to assist the domestic implementation of FDIQR-aligned commitments on sustainable investment. International organisations can rely on a combination of technical assistance and capacity building measures to identify gaps in IIA implementation and guide domestic reform efforts in alignment with treaty commitments. Treaties in the IIA sample also recognise the importance of co-operating with international organisations. Notably, the WTO IFD Agreement calls for increased collaboration and co-ordination with international organisations in the provision of technical assistance and capacity building to developing countries and LDCs (Article 36.5 and Article 36.6).

Several organisations have developed specialised tools and methodologies to review and improve domestic investment frameworks. The World Bank Group supports the development of FDI Strategies and Investment Roadmaps, improvements of policy effectiveness, promotion of good practices and the strengthening of investor confidence (World Bank Group, 2022[9]). UNCTAD carries out country reviews to provide strategic advice to governments on how to attract and benefit from foreign direct investment (FDI) (UNCTAD, 2008[10]) The OECD also relies on several tools to support investment climate reforms in beneficiary countries. A first instrument is the Investment Policy Review (IPR), a country-specific report that benchmarks the local investment and business climate against the principles of the OECD Policy Framework for Investment, 2015 Edition (PFI) (OECD, 2015[11]). The PFI, last updated in 2015, takes a whole-of-government approach to investment climate reform and is the most comprehensive and systematic multilateral-backed instrument for improving investment conditions ever developed. It is a non-prescriptive, flexible instrument, that emphasises policy coherence and results in policy advice that is tailored to both the domestic and international context.

IPRs are developed by the OECD in partnership with the government of the beneficiary country. They evaluate progress and priorities for actions in 12 policy areas covered by the PFI. All IPRs include chapters on the entry, regulation and protection of investment, investment promotion and facilitation, and responsible business conduct. Other policy areas (e.g. competition, trade, tax, corporate governance, human resource development, finance, infrastructure, public governance and channelling investment into areas that promote green growth) can be also included, depending on the wishes and priorities of the government undertaking the review. To date, IPRs have been used by over 40 states, at varying levels of development and across all continents, as a tool for assessing investment and business climates, and for designing reforms to improve them. Recently published IPRs include Egypt, Indonesia, Thailand, and Viet Nam, with ongoing reviews in Bangladesh, Morocco and Uzbekistan and planned reviews in Guatemala, Moldova and Zambia.

More recently, the OECD launched a new methodological instrument, based on the FDIQR and related Policy Toolkit, to complement the PFI-based analysis of the IPRs. The FDI Qualities Reviews provide tailored policy advice to the beneficiary government on how to strengthen the impact of FDI on four sustainability-related areas: (i) productivity and innovation; (ii) jobs and skills development, including for local SMEs; (iii) gender equality; and (iv) decarbonisation. The areas of focus are chosen in agreement with the government, in alignment with national development objectives and priorities. The FDI Qualities Reviews complement the IPR analysis by providing governments with detailed guidance on how to influence and improve the quality of investment, going beyond investment climate reform. They include evidence-based analysis of FDI's impact on the selected sustainability areas and of how existing strategies, policies and institutions can support investment contributing to the identified priorities. They also set out policy recommendations to align investment and sustainable development objectives. To date, FDI Qualities Reviews have been undertaken, in general or for specific sustainable areas, with Austria, Croatia, Chile, Ireland, Jordan, and Tunisia. Additional FDI Qualities Reviews are ongoing in Canada, Egypt, and Viet Nam.

The processes for the implementation of tools and methodologies designed to improve domestic investment frameworks varies across organisations. Looking specifically at IPRs and FDI Qualities reviews, their process follows a set of standardised steps, broadly divided into three phases (Figure 4.4).

Figure 4.4. Implementing the IPR/FDI Qualities Review process

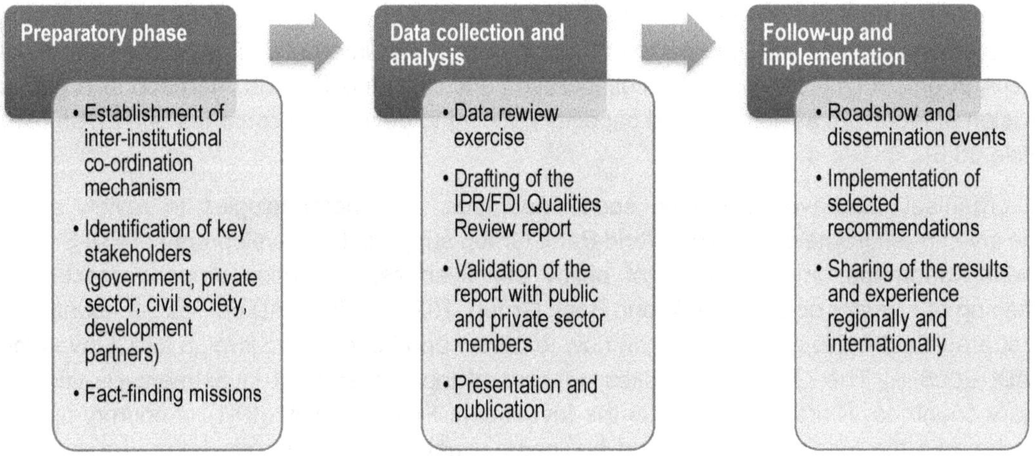


Source: OECD adapted from the description of FDI Qualities Review and IPR process.

### *4.3.1. Developing the IPRs and FDI Qualities Review reports*

The first step consists of the preparation of the IPR/FDI Qualities Review process, which includes co-ordination with relevant stakeholders and the implementation of fact-finding missions. The OECD then prepares the relevant report through activities of data gathering and analysis. Consultations are also undertaken with interested stakeholders within the public and the private sector, for the purpose of validating findings and recommendation. Such a process has recently been implemented in Croatia, with the publication of the FDI Qualities Review of Croatia in November 2023 (Box 4.3).

**Box 4.3. The FDI Qualities Review process and timeline: The Croatia example**

Between April 2022 and December 2023, with the financial assistance of the European Union, the OECD developed an FDI Qualities Review to support the government of Croatia in advancing its strategic framework for promoting and facilitating private investments.

**Preparatory phase: Co-ordination and fact-finding activities**

*July 2022.* The OECD and the Croatian Ministry of Economy and Sustainable Development (MESD), as lead government agency, establish an inter-institutional Working Group, whose mandate includes facilitating policy dialogue among public and private sector stakeholders, ensuring information exchange, and co-ordinating intermediate and final outputs.

*September 2022.* An OECD team of experts conducts a fact-finding mission to Croatia, where it meets with government representatives at the central and local level, as well as representatives of the private sector and international organisations, to identify and discuss the main challenges and opportunities for private investment in Croatia.

**Data collection and analysis: Preparation and validation of the FDI Qualities Review report**

*October 2022-January 2023*. The OECD drafts the FDI Qualities report, based on a desk-based analysis of Croatia's business and investment climate and available information on investment promotion policies, surveys addressed to relevant institutional actors, and meetings with the MESD.

*January 2023*. The OECD submits a first version of the FDI Qualities Review report to the MESD. The report: (i) assesses how FDI contributes to productivity and innovation, job quality and skills development, decarbonisation, and regional development in Croatia; (ii) examines the institutional and policy framework for investment promotion and facilitation at national and subnational levels; (iii) analyses Croatia's investment incentives regime; and (iv) sets out potential areas for institutional and policy reform to improve Croatia's investment climate and strengthen benefits of FDI.

*May 2023*. The OECD presents preliminary findings and recommendations of the FDI Qualities Review report in four consultation workshops with public and private sector stakeholders, organised in collaboration with the MESD. The FDI Qualities Reviews report is updated based on comments received.

*November 2023*. The OECD officially publishes the FDI Qualities Reviews of Croatia during a public event organised in co-operation with the MESD and the European Union. The event gathered more than 120 participants, including government representatives at the local and central level, members of the private sector and EU delegates.

Source: OECD data; (OECD, 2023[12])

### *4.3.2. Implementing the IPR and FDI Qualities Review recommendations*

The process for an IPR or FDI Qualities Review does not stop with the publication of the relevant report. It can also include active support in the follow-up phase, with the provision of technical assistance in implementing relevant recommendations and adopting measures to improve the national investment climate. The support can extend to assisting in drafting coherent and integrated national policies, strategies or action plans related to sustainable investment, as well as of investment-related laws and regulations, with a view to ensuring proper consideration to sustainable development concerns. It can also include the provision of capacity building to support the implementation of recommendations, such as developing capacity for the IPA operations. More recently, the OECD has provided technical assistance in the follow up to the FDI Qualities Reviews of Croatia and Jordan, for example (Box 4.4).

**Box 4.4. The follow-up to the FDI Qualities Reviews process: Selected country examples**

**Supporting the review of the draft Investment Promotion Act of Croatia**

The OECD provided technical advice and targeted feedback on the draft amendments to the Act on Investment Promotion prepared by the MESD. The OECD's technical input focused on recommendations to revise legal provisions related to the use of financial incentives to support the green transition. Additional recommendations were also provided on aspects related to defining the types of eligible investment projects and the specific criteria that should apply. This feedback helped to further align the draft amendments with the recommendations of the FDI Qualities Review of Croatia.

**Providing technical advice on the draft Investment Environment Law of Jordan**

In June 2022, the OECD launched the FDI Qualities Review of Jordan. The report analysed, among other things, the impact of the 2014 Investment Law of Jordan on jobs and skills development, highlighting the importance of aligning policy objectives on investment and employment in the context of ongoing law reform processes. On this basis, in the follow-up to the publication of the report, the OECD was invited to provide comments to the draft of the new investment law and further streamline investment and sustainability objectives, including in the area of jobs creation and skills development. Jordan's new Investment Environment Law entered into force in September 2022, contributing to align the domestic investment climate with sustainability objectives.

Source: (OECD, 2022[13]; OECD, 2023[12]).

### *4.3.3. Evaluating the effectiveness of the IPR and FDI Qualities Review process*

OECD reviews of investment policies are sometimes evaluated *ex post*. Evaluations are of key importance to assess whether the support received from international organisations is effectively leading to an improved investment climate in the beneficiary states. Independent evaluations have highlighted the effectiveness of the IPRs implemented by the OECD in support of ASEAN member states (Box 4.5). Among the success factors, the adoption of a whole of government and a modular approach to investment climate assessment were mentioned. In addition, independent evaluations also noted how the analysis and recommendations emerging from the IPR process were key in facilitating exchanges of best practices and lessons learned, fostering a better understanding of investment policy tools and approaches (ASEAN, 2020[14]).

**Box 4.5. Evaluating the impact of IPR processes in the ASEAN region**

Between 2013 and 2018, the OECD undertook IPRs in six ASEAN countries: Malaysia, Myanmar, the Philippines, Lao PDR, Viet Nam, and Cambodia. The IPRs were undertaken under the umbrella of the ASEAN-Australia-New Zealand FTA (AANZFTA) Economic Cooperation Support Programme (AECSP), with a view to strengthening ASEAN's investment climate and operationalising the commitments arising under the AANZFTA. The AECSP conducted a thorough evaluation of the IPR process to assess to what extent it had achieved the desired objectives, highlighting that the IPR process:

- Improved investment reform governance by providing a platform for continuous dialogue among stakeholders and guiding efforts to strengthen national policies and public institutions.
- Increased the transparency in developing investment policies, providing information and clarity to policymakers from different ministries and agencies and improving engagement with the private sector.
- Strengthened partnership with development partners and improved on-the-ground co-ordination to ensure support in implementing the recommendations included in the IPR.
- Increased stakeholders' understanding of the latest developments and best practices on investment in ASEAN member states.

The evaluation noted how, in several cases, the policy recommendations included in the IPRs led to the adoption of legislative or institutional reforms, as well as the implementation of new measures. In this context, it highlighted how the IPRs provided an objective view of necessary reforms and contributed to the implementation of solutions in accordance with international best practices and domestic objectives.

Source: (ASEAN, 2020[14]).

#### 4.3.4. Implications for domestic implementation

Benchmarking tools and methodologies developed by international organisations can play a key role in supporting the domestic implementation of FDIQR-aligned commitments on sustainable development. They can support the parties in the identification of implementation gaps in implementation and recommend potential measures that states could put in place at the domestic level in compliance with their international commitments. International organisations can also support state parties through the provision of dedicated technical assistance and capacity building to facilitate implementation, including by harnessing resources available under development co-operation.

Looking at the instruments and methodologies developed specifically by the OECD, the IPR and FDI Qualities Review processes offer a flexible instrument that address many of the elements already included FDIQ-aligned international commitments on sustainable investment, making them particularly suitable to support domestic implementation.

### 4.4. Harnessing development co-operation and international partnerships

Development co-operation is a key resource to mobilise FDI. Especially in developing countries and LDCs, it can help reduce barriers to investment and lower risk perceptions that prevent these countries from harnessing FDI, including by supporting effective investment climate reforms at the domestic level. The FDIQR also recognises the importance of development co-operation through the following two dedicated principles:

- **FDIQR principle 5.a, Technical assistance and capacity building**: Identify ways that financial and technical assistance can support the implementation of the FDIQR to enhance the impact of FDI on sustainable development.
- **FDIQR principle 5.b, Development co-operation**: Promote alignment of donors' assistance with national priorities related to sustainable investment in accordance with relevant international standards, including through the mapping of such assistance, and the identification of potential support gaps or opportunities to replicate or scale-up existing assistance.

To support the implementation of such principles, the OECD developed the FDI Qualities Guide for Development Cooperation (the Guide), which provides specific guidance to donors and other development co-operation actors on strengthening the role of development co-operation in mobilising FDI and enhancing its positive impacts in developing countries (OECD, 2022[15]). The Guide provides examples of technical and financial solutions that can enhance the impact of FDI on sustainable development and sets out principles that can guide donors in designing, implementing, and monitoring FDI-related assistance.

Beyond broad support on FDI mobilisation, development co-operation can be harnessed for the implementation of specific FDIQR-aligned IIA commitments on sustainable investment. Donor resources could be used to support international organisations in providing technical assistance and capacity building to national institutions in implementing domestic reform processes seeking to strengthen the investment climate in alignment with international commitments.

#### 4.4.1. Development co-operation for the implementation of IIA commitments

Treaties within the IIA sample include references to the role that development co-operation can play in their implementation. The Investment Protocol to the AfCFTA provides for a specific obligation of state parties to "support the provision of technical assistance, capacity building and co-operation" to promote and facilitate investment under the agreement and, for this purpose, to co-ordinate with the Agency and the AfCFTA Secretariat (Article 43). Under the EU-Angola SIFA, the parties "recognise the importance of technical assistance and capacity-building and commit to co-operate on strengthening the investment climate in Angola" and supporting the implementation of the agreement. Notably, the agreement explicitly recognises that the assistance should be undertaken within the framework of the EU's development co-operation initiatives and partnerships (Article 42).

A different understanding of development co-operation – as flowing from "donor" treaty parties to "beneficiary" treaty parties – permeates instead the WTO IFD Agreement. Donor countries party to the treaty commit to "facilitate the provision of technical assistance and support" to beneficiary parties to assist them in their implementation efforts, either through bilateral arrangements or through the channel of international organisations (Article 35.1). The agreement also identifies examples of what technical assistance and capacity building may entail, including strengthening the capacity of governmental authorities to maximise positive impacts of investment and building capacity for the preparation of feasibility studies for investment projects (Article 35.5).

There are several ways in which development co-operation can support IIA implementation, whether in the context of existing strategic partnerships or otherwise. It could, for example:

- Support domestic reform efforts, in line with international treaty commitments and the results of needs assessment processes carried out by international organisations. This can entail, for example, technical support and capacity building in developing policies that can foster the positive impacts of FDI. It can also extend to the provision of financial and budget support, to ensure policy continuity and the achievement of the sustainable investment objectives pursued through domestic reform efforts.
- Facilitate the design of legal frameworks aligned with sustainable development objectives, in line with IIA requirements. Technical support can be directed towards developing new laws or regulations that may be required pursuant to relevant treaty commitments and building the capacity of relevant institutions to implement relevant legislation.
- Assist a treaty party in meeting cross-border regulatory requirements on investment applicable in the other treaty party. A typical example is that of taxonomy regulations on sustainable investment, such as the one first adopted in the European Union. Without adequate support, partner developing countries and LDCs may struggle to find the resources and technical and institutional capacity to comply with relevant standards.
- Contribute to the further development of monitoring and evaluation processes seeking to measure the impacts of FDI on sustainable development, which is crucial in determining the effectiveness of state initiatives on sustainable investment. It can also support efforts to harmonise environmental, social and governance (ESG) frameworks, contributing to the development of comparable and clear ESG standards. In both cases, the support could entail, for example, the provision of technical assistance in developing metrics and indicators, data collection efforts, and establishing monitoring systems, as well as exchanges of best practices in the area.
- Contribute to operationalising programmes and initiatives in line with the FDIQR principles, for example on investment promotion and facilitation. This can entail, among other things, the provision of funding for specific skills development programmes or other initiatives linking foreign investors with local employees or building the capacity of the local workforce in specific sustainability-related areas (e.g. decarbonisation, gender equality). Financial support could also be directed towards the establishment and implementation of suppliers development programmes, to build the capacity of domestic firms to become partners and suppliers of foreign investors. Development co-operation could also help build the capacity of investment promotion agencies to prioritise investment against specific sustainability criteria and delivering services to businesses in a way that maximises the positive contribution of investment to sustainable development.

More broadly, development co-operation can support developing countries and LDCs in negotiating IIAs aligned with sustainable development objectives. Developing countries and LDCs face significant challenges when it comes to IIA negotiation, often linked to lack or insufficiency of human, financial and technical resources to properly engage in the negotiation process (OECD, 2022[15]). Technical assistance from donor countries, including in the form of capacity building, can help developing countries negotiate agreements that reflect national priorities and objectives on sustainable investment and that already incorporate tools and mechanisms to support their own implementation at the domestic level, including through the establishment of institutional co-operation mechanisms.

### *4.4.2. Principles guiding development co-operation for IIA implementation*

To be truly effective, development co-operation must be deployed in accordance with clear prioritisation strategies, considering also the specific country contexts and objectives (OECD, 2022[15]). The FDI Qualities Guide for Development Cooperation sets out six key principles that can help strengthen the effectiveness of development co-operation in enhancing the impacts of FDI on sustainable development. While these principles are general in nature, they may become relevant also for the delivery of development co-operation initiatives for the implementation of IIAs.

The Guide sets out the following principles:

1. **Assessing and understanding the impacts of FDI on sustainable development in a given context**. The Guide recognises that, to effectively design and implement support measures to enhance sustainable investment, it is essential to examine the relationship between FDI and sustainable development in the specific country context. The assessment of the impacts of FDI on sustainable development is especially important in the context of IIA implementation, as it can support the identification of the priorities and objectives to be achieved through development co-operation initiatives.
2. **Ensuring alignment with national priorities**. The Guide recognises that development co-operation initiatives on investment and sustainable development should be informed and aligned with countries' national priorities. The same principle finds explicit recognition in recent IIAs on investment facilitation for sustainable development. The EU-Angola SIFA, for example, clarifies that technical assistance and capacity building initiatives are to be carried out in the context of the EU's development co-operation framework, and that relevant requests for assistance should be aligned with identified needs and domestic investment reform priorities (Article 42, para 2). When looking at IIA implementation, this principle entails that potential development co-operation initiatives should be tailored to the specific country context, aligned with specific sustainable investment priorities, and should take into account ongoing reform efforts, with a view to avoid duplications and inconsistencies.
3. **Ensuring co-ordination and coherence among the development co-operation community**. Building on the 2005 Paris Declaration on Aid Effectiveness, this principle recognises that several development co-operation partners may provide investment-related support in a given country, potentially leading to overlap and duplication of activities and inconsistencies in reform efforts, prejudicing the effectiveness of development co-operation. The importance of inter-agency and donor co-ordination in development co-operation is recognised also in the WTO IFD Agreement, which stresses the importance of promoting co-ordination between member states and other relevant institutions "to ensure maximum effectiveness of and results from" the envisaged assistance (Article 35.3, letter (d)).
4. **Identifying trade-offs and complementarities and managing risks**. Development actors should consider trade-offs and complementarities that may exist between the support modalities to which they have recourse, as well as between the specific sustainable development objectives that they are seeking to pursue. Development co-operation partners should also try to identify and manage potential unintended consequences of their interventions, particularly with respect to domestic firms or the creation of market distortions.

5. **Engaging with businesses, trade unions and civil society. Involving stakeholders in the design and implementation of development co-operation initiatives is key to maximise their effectiveness.** This is especially relevant when it comes to sustainable investment, as domestic reforms to be implemented under the umbrella of relevant IIAs are generally aimed at improving the investment climate in a way that benefits businesses, workers, and civil society alike. Recent IIAs also stress the role of the private sector in shaping development co-operation initiatives for the improvement of the domestic investment climate. For example, the WTO IFD Agreement highlights the importance of ensuring that private sector-led investment facilitation reform initiatives are taken into account into prospective development co-operation initiatives (Article 35.3, letter (c)).
6. **Enhancing impact measurement and accountability**. The Guide highlights the importance of adequate impact measurement, transparency, and accountability in ensuring that development co-operation initiatives achieve their intended objectives, while at the same time promoting effectiveness and trust. This principle is connected to the need to ensure effective monitoring and evaluation of development co-operation interventions, measuring them against desired results. More generally, monitoring and evaluation activities undertaken in this context could also contribute to determining whether IIA provisions have been properly implemented. In general, the Guide notes how there is significant scope to enhance monitoring and evaluation capacities linked with development co-operation initiatives. On this topic, the WTO IFD Agreement highlights the importance of relying on existing in-country and regional co-ordination structures (e.g. roundtables, consultative groups) to co-ordinate and monitor implementation activities (Article 35.3, letter (e)).

## 4.5. Applying the implementation framework: Conclusions and potential way forward

FDIQR-aligned IIA commitments on sustainable investment have very peculiar features. They are positive in nature, as they require an active conduct from the state party in the form of the adoption of measures to implement treaty commitments. They can produce widespread benefits, as improvements in the investment climate prompted by the adoption of relevant measures ultimately have beneficial consequences not only for investors of the other party, but for all foreign and domestic investors. Because the benefits they give are widespread, in case of non-compliance, the remedy of compensation traditionally associated with the breach of IIA provisions may be less appropriate. In these cases, the focus should be placed in ensuring that the state adopts the measures required under the breached commitment, thus leading to an effective improvement of the investment climate.

All these specificities inevitably influence their implementation, requiring the development of a new framework that seeks to facilitate parties' compliance with international commitments on sustainable investment, rather than sanctioning instances of non-compliance. Such an implementation framework relies on three main tools: reporting and information exchange, financial assistance, and technical assistance, including capacity building. These tools can be harnessed through three different implementation mechanisms: treaty-based institutional co-operation mechanisms; support from international organisations; and development co-operation. In practice, the way in which these tools and co-operation mechanisms interact will vary depending on the different stages of the IIA process, and in particular on whether an IIA is already in place or not.

### *4.5.1. Facilitating the implementation of existing IIAs*

The application of the implementation framework to existing IIAs is straightforward and can be better understood by taking the EU-Angola SIFA as an example (Figure 4.5). The choice of analysing the EU-Angola SIFA can be justified due to the high number of sustainable investment-related commitments that it includes, its bilateral nature, and the circumstance that it makes an explicit reference to two out of three co-operation mechanisms considered in the implementation framework, namely the recourse to institutional co-operation mechanisms and reliance on development co-operation.

While both the European Union and Angola bear the primary responsibility for the implementation of their commitments under the EU-Angola SIFA, they can first rely on treaty-based institutional co-operation mechanisms to support and facilitate their respective implementation efforts. The EU-Angola SIFA establishes a Committee on Investment Facilitation (Article 43), tasked with supervising and facilitating the implementation of relevant treaty commitments (Article 44). For this purpose, the Committee can adopt recommendations in respect of all matters covered by SIFA, , as well as binding decisions “where provided for in [the agreement]”. The parties could harness the powers attributed to the Committee on Investment Facilitation to support implementation efforts. For example, while specific reporting or information exchange obligations are not specifically envisaged in the EU-Angola SIFA, the Committee could recommend that the parties periodically submit reports detailing progress in the implementation of the treaty, included measures adopted. The provision of information in this area would facilitate monitoring efforts, as well as the identification of gaps in implementation. In particular, it could be possible for the Committee to recommend to the parties specific technical or financial support interventions that would be beneficial to assist in implementing SIFA commitments.

Treaty parties, either independently or in the context of their co-operation in the Committee on Investment Facilitation, could seek development co-operation support, as made available under the EU framework. Resources granted to the parties can be used to implement technical assistance and capacity building programmes conducive to the implementation of the SIFA (Article 42), as well to support domestic reform processes. Development co-operation resources could also be harnessed to enlist international organisations in supporting the implementation of international commitments. For example, such resources could be used to support sustainable investment areas where parties have identified gaps or opportunities for priority interventions.

Figure 4.5. Implementing an existing IIA: The EU-Angola SIFA example

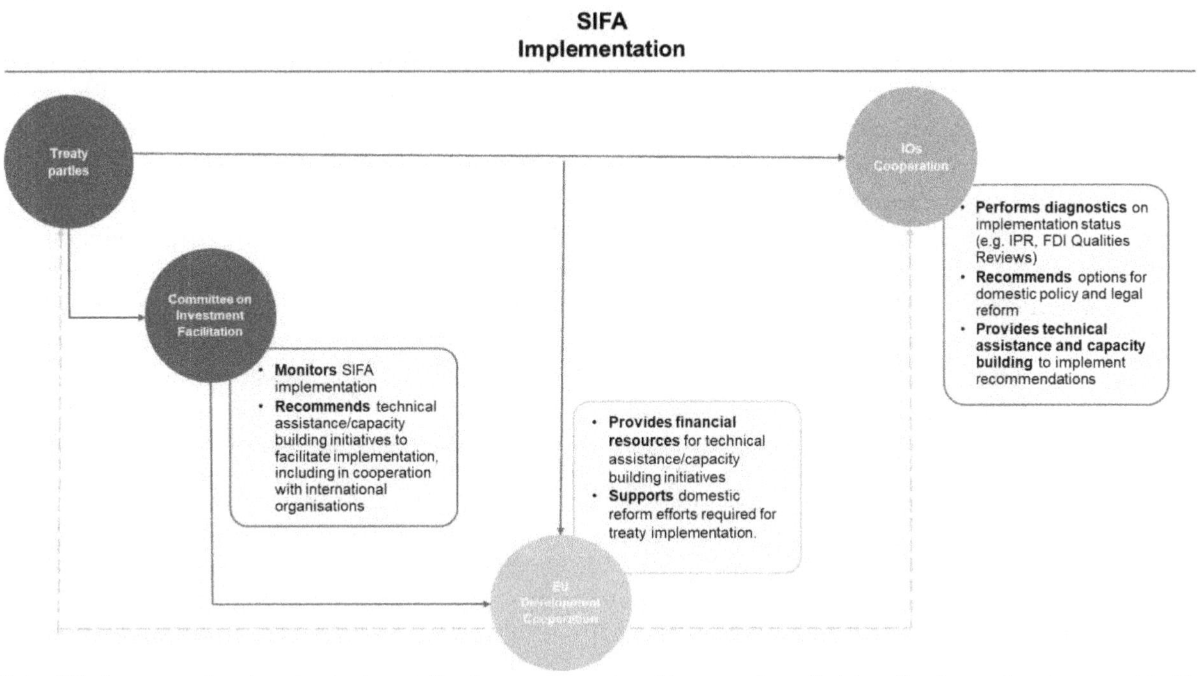


Note: This figure examines how the implementation framework developed in connection with international commitments on sustainable investment could be applied to the implementation of the EU-Angola SIFA, and in particular be harnessed to support Angola in its efforts to implement relevant treaty commitments at the domestic level. The dotted green lines show the direction in the disbursement of funds from EU development co-operation, while the blue lines show the requests for support that can be issued by treaty parties.
Source: OECD, based on the implementation framework.

Regardless of the initiative of the Committee on Investment Facilitation under the EU-Angola SIFA, the parties would remain free to seek the support of international organisations of their own accord. In the implementation of SIFA-like agreements, international organisations could play a key role in the preparation of a gap analysis or needs assessment study on the parties' legal and policy frameworks on investment, with a view to identifying areas where domestic reforms are needed. The support could also extend to the provision of technical assistance and capacity building in the implementation of relevant recommendations under the study (Box 4.6).

### Box 4.6. Gap analysis of Angola's legal framework on sustainable investment for the implementation of the EU-Angola SIFA

A gap analysis of Angola's legal and policy framework could help assess the country's level of alignment with international principles on sustainable investment, identifying areas where further action might be required in the implementation of relevant IIA commitments.

To better illustrate how such a gap analysis might work in practice, the examples below provide a high-level assessment concerning the alignment between Angola's legal framework with selected principles of the FDI Qualities Recommendation. It will also provide high-level examples of how such an alignment may impact the implementation of relevant commitments under the EU-Angola SIFA.

- **FDIQR principle 1.d, Impact assessment**: Angola has a legal framework on Environmental and Social Impact Assessment (ESIA) in line with international standards. A gap analysis focusing on the ESIA law would therefore focus on challenges in implementing relevant legislation at the domestic level and how they affect the implementation of investment projects in Angola, to be assessed through interviews with selected stakeholders. At the same time, it does not appear that Angola has enacted legislation on Strategic Environmental Assessment (SEA) for policies, plans and programmes. If the lack of SEA legislation were to be confirmed through stakeholder interviews, domestic action in this area would, therefore, be required, to ensure compliance with relevant provisions under the EU-Angola SIFA.
- **FDIQR principle 2.b, Domestic alignment between investment and gender objectives.** Angola's National Development Plan (NDP) 2023-2027 includes specific objectives concerning the achievement of gender equality in economic activities. The NDP seeks to promote women's economic empowerment through targeted action, involving, among other things, promoting women's access to finance, providing training courses to women on small business management and entrepreneurship, providing financial education services, and monitoring the representation of women in the different employment and entrepreneurship projects. In 2018, Angola also adopted a Strategy for Investment Promotion and Attraction, which does not appear to be publicly available. A gap analysis in this area would allow to determine the level to which the Strategy for Investment Promotion and Attraction considers gender-related concerns and to formulate recommendations on how to ensure increased consistency between the two areas, in compliance with relevant provisions under the EU-Angola SIFA.
- **FDIQR principle 4.b and 4.c, Investment Promotion and Facilitation**. Since 2020, AIPEX, Angola's investment promotion agency, manages the Single Investment Windows (*Janela Unica de Investimento*), which is aimed at simplifying contacts between foreign investors and public entities involved in the approval of foreign investment projects. Publicly available information on investment promotion and facilitation activities, especially in support of specific sustainability objectives, are scarce. A gap analysis would allow to take direct contact with governmental authorities to obtain more information on this matter, thus gaining insights on the measures that the investment promotion agency is implementing to promote and facilitate sustainable investment at the domestic level, in alignment with commitments under the EU-Angola SIFA.

Source: For ESIA, Law No. 5/98, Basic Environmental Law and Presidential Decree No. 117/20, General Regulation for Environmental impact Assessment and Environmental Licensing Procedure; for the NDP 2023-2027, https://www.mep.gov.ao/assets/indicadores/angola2050/20231030(3)_layout_Final_Angola_PDN%202023-2027-1.pdf; for the Single Investment Window, https://www.aipex.gov.ao/PortalAIPEX/#!/destaques/setip.

### *4.5.2. Facilitating the negotiation and implementation of future IIAs*

Applied to the negotiation and implementation of future IIAs, including SIFAs, the implementation framework offers additional opportunities for interactions between the three different implementation mechanisms (Figure 4.6). To ensure consistency with the previous section, the analysis will take as example the negotiation of a future SIFA-like agreement, that the European Union may wish to negotiate in the future. This exercise could also be done for any other possible future agreement with sustainable investment objectives.

Parties that may wish to engage in the negotiation of a future SIFA-like arrangement could seek immediate recourse to development co-operation. The support provided could be twofold. First, development co-operation resources could be directed towards the strengthening of state parties' capacity to negotiate IIAs themselves, enhancing government officials' skills to identify domestic negotiation priorities objectives and red lines and to adopt specific negotiation strategies. Such type of support could be provided through the involvement of relevant international organisations, thus contributing to the dissemination and uptake of best practices in IIAs negotiation and leading to better negotiation outcomes in the future. For example, it could support the inclusion in the future SIFA-like commitments in line with sustainable investment, as well as of provisions establishing institutional co-operation mechanisms with powers to effectively support and facilitate domestic implementation.

Development co-operation, however, could also facilitate broader investment climate reform processes, regardless of the involvement in an IIA negotiation. Efforts to improve the investment climate at the domestic level undertaken in the pre-negotiation phase could also contribute to ease the implementation of future SIFA commitments. Also in this case, support could be provided through the involvement of relevant international organisations. Their involvement could support the development of a gap analysis concerning the alignment of the existing legal and policy framework with sustainable development objectives, as well as in the provision of technical assistance and capacity building in the implementation of relevant recommendations. At the same time,

The same type of support could be provided also following the signature of the new SIFA-like agreement, thereby supporting its implementation. In this case, the options available to treaty parties and the interactions among different implementation mechanisms would follow the analysis already outlined in the previous section. In particular, the Committee on Investment Facilitation envisaged under the new SIFA would be able to exercise oversight and facilitation functions over the implementation of the agreement, activating, where necessary, recourse to development co-operation and support from international organisations in facilitating investment climate reforms in accordance with international commitments.

## Figure 4.6. Implementing a future IIA: The example of other SIFA-like agreement

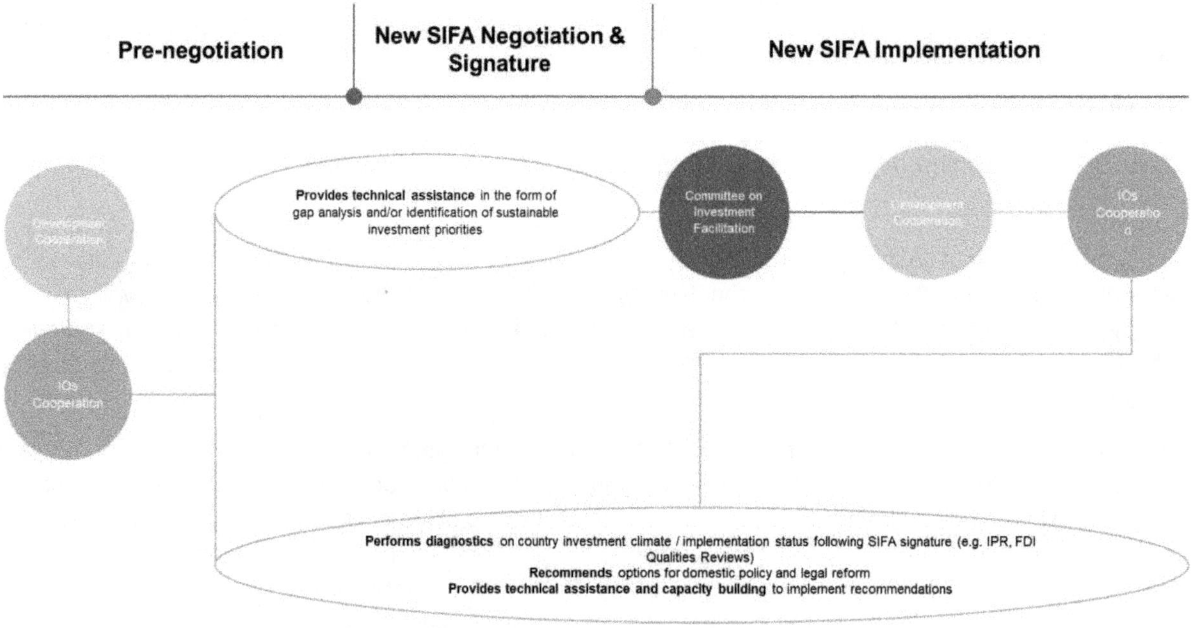


Note: This figure examines how the implementation framework developed in connection with international commitments on sustainable investment could be applied to the implementation of future SIFA-like agreements that the European Union may wish to enter into with third countries. The red line in the timeline represents the signature of the new SIFA-like treaty, thus distinguishing the pre-negotiation and negotiation phases from implementation.
Source: OECD, based on the implementation framework.

## References


ASEAN (2020), *Investment Policy for Sustainable Development in the AANZFTA Region*, https://aanzfta.asean.org/uploads/2020/08/Investment%20Policy%20for%20Sustainable%20Development%20in%20the%20AANZFTA%20Region_Final%20Res.pdf. [14]

Bodansky, D. (2010), *The art and craft of international environmental law*, Harvard University Press. [1]

Dupuy, P. and J. Viñuales (2018), *International Environmental Law*, Cambridge University Press, https://doi.org/10.1017/9781108399821. [3]

Gordon, K. and J. Pohl (2015), “Investment Treaties over Time - Treaty Practice and Interpretation in a Changing World”, *OECD Working Papers on International Investment*, No. 2015/2, OECD Publishing, Paris, https://doi.org/10.1787/5js7rhd8sq7h-en. [2]

IISD (2024), *Investment Facilitation for Development Agreement: A reader’s guide*, https://www.iisd.org/system/files/2024-02/investment-facilitation-development-agreement-wto.pdf. [6]

International Trade Center and World Economic Forum (2024), *Report on the 7th capacity building workshop on “Making use of the WTO’s Investment Facilitation for Development Agreement for attracting sustainable and inclusive FDI”*, https://intracen.org/sites/default/files/inline-files/IF%2C%20WTO%20IISD%20event%2C%20Feb.%2024%2C%20Report_FINAL%20for%20publication.pdf. [4]

ODI (2023), *AfCFTA National Implementatio Committees: Scoping options and support mechanisms*, https://media.odi.org/documents/ODI-AfCFTA-Report-18Apr23-FINAL.pdf. [7]

OECD (2023), *FDI Qualities Review of Croatia: Advancing the Strategic Framework for Investment Promotion and Facilitation*, OECD Publishing, Paris, https://doi.org/10.1787/79b2345b-en. [12]

OECD (2022), *FDI Qualities Guide for Development Co-operation: Strengthening the Role of Development Co-operation for Sustainable Investment*, OECD Development Policy Tools, OECD Publishing, Paris, https://doi.org/10.1787/7f251bac-en. [15]

OECD (2022), *FDI Qualities Policy Toolkit*, OECD Publishing, Paris, https://doi.org/10.1787/7ba74100-en. [8]

OECD (2022), *FDI Qualities Review of Jordan: Strengthening Sustainable Investment*, OECD Publishing, Paris, https://doi.org/10.1787/736c77d2-en. [13]

OECD (2015), *Policy Framework for Investment, 2015 Edition*, OECD Publishing, Paris, https://doi.org/10.1787/9789264208667-en. [11]

UNCTAD (2008), *The Investment Policy Reviews Programme: A Framework for Attracting and Benefitting from FDI*, https://unctad.org/system/files/official-document/iteipc20083_en.pdf. [10]

World Bank Group (2022), *Investment Policy and Promotion: Attracting Foreign Investment and Maximizing Impact for the Local Economy*, https://documents1.worldbank.org/curated/en/099040009302225750/pdf/P1755370c5dafe0440b2e40efcc6443b101.pdf. [9]

World Trade Organization (2023), *WTO Technical Assistance Annual Report*, https://www.wto.org/english/tratop_e/devel_e/teccop_e/ta_annrep23_e.pdf. [5]

# 5 Options for the incorporation of commitments on sustainable investment in the negotiation of international investment agreements

This chapter analyses how future international investment agreements (IIAs) can further align with selected principles of the FDI Qualities Recommendation (FDIQR). It introduces two options for the introduction of new provisions on sustainable investment in the context of IIA negotiation: one based on the introduction of treaty language that builds on existing treaty provisions already in line with the FDIQR, and one that relies on parties' co-operation in the implementation of relevant IIAs provisions.

## 5.1. Possible options for the inclusion of new provisions on sustainable investment in the negotiation of international investment agreements

This chapter explores potential options to introduce new provisions on sustainable investment in the context of IIA negotiation, to strengthen alignment between IIAs and sustainable investment objectives in the above identified FDI Qualities areas. The negotiation process allows the parties to reflect and agree on a shared set of values to which they commit, and to identify the most appropriate tools and approaches that can be used in the achievement of their common objectives. Since IIA commitments will have to be implemented domestically – with potential consequences associated with non-compliance – the negotiation will have to strike a balance between the commitments themselves and the ability of states to deliver on them.

There are two practices emerging from the analysis of the IIA sample that appear to advance the incorporation of sustainable investment-related elements in IIAs. The first relies on the incorporation of substantive provisions on sustainable investment. The second, instead, relies on institutional co-operation mechanisms formulated in IIAs. Both approaches will be considered in the analysis of how the FDIQR principles identified above can be better integrated in future IIAs.

Concerning the first practice, the analysis of substantive language will be based on existing IIA provisions already aligned with the FDIQR, as identified in the stocktaking exercise under Chapter 2. Suggestions on potential amendments or edits to existing language will be, instead, based on the review of domestic practices carried out in Chapter 3. It is important to highlight that the analysis of potential substantive language is neither prescriptive nor exhaustive. It only provides an opportunity of reflection on how to better reconcile investment and sustainable development objectives.

In addition, there might be also additional substantive language – other than those emerging from the sample of reviewed IIAs or domestic practices – that can contribute to the strengthening of sustainable investment considerations in IIAs. In general, how treaty language on sustainable investment is drafted in practice will depend on the negotiating parties' choices. There are several elements that will influence the decision, including the type of treaty to be negotiated (e.g. a BIT versus an FTA versus a SIFA-like agreement), the specific objectives and priorities of the negotiating parties, the negotiating context and the parties' own negotiation practices, and the features of the parties' own domestic legal and regulatory framework.

Concerning the second practice, while this is mostly focused on the parties' co-operation in the context of IIA-based joint committees, it is important to recall that the other implementation mechanisms envisaged under the methodological framework under Chapter 4 may also play an important role in supporting the parties' joint initiatives. Co-operation initiatives identified by the parties in the context of joint committees or other treaty bodies can be, therefore, complemented and supported by development co-operation or by the initiatives of relevant international organisations.

Before proceeding further with the analysis, the following clarifications are also necessary:

- *Consideration of the broader context.* IIAs are not the only policy instrument available to states to foster sustainable investment. The specific country context in the negotiating state – including its investment and sustainable development priorities and its own capacity and level of development – will inevitably affect the choice of the policy instruments that are the most appropriate to achieve the desired objectives. The same context will also influence the state's own negotiation approach to future IIAs. The decision on which sustainable investment commitments to include in the IIA may be influenced in part by what the state has done or plans to do domestically to harness sustainable investment.
- *Consideration related to the IIA type.* The type of IIA the parties are negotiating will also influence the choice of the negotiation approach. For example, Free Trade Agreements (FTAs) have a much broader scope compared to traditional Bilateral Investment Treaties, also covering areas such as

regulatory coherence or sustainable development in specific chapters (different than the investment chapters). Hence, they offer more opportunities for the integration of sustainable investment concerns. International green economy collaborations such as the Singapore-Australia Green Economy Agreement (GEA) have not only a very focused scope – addressing the issue of decarbonisation specifically – but are also entirely non-binding. They provide a framework for the parties' co-operation, without creating binding commitments. All these specificities may have an impact on the choice of negotiating approach that is more appropriate in a given context.

- *Consideration of implementation needs*. IIA commitments will have to be implemented domestically. The level of ambition under the IIA will have to take into account the specific financial, human, and technical resources at the state's disposal. Such elements may therefore also influence the choice of negotiating approach, with reliance on co-operation being, in certain instances, more appropriate than the introduction of new treaty commitments.

## 5.2. Examining treaty negotiation approaches in selected FDI Qualities areas

### *5.2.1. FDIQR principle 1.d: Assessment and periodic review of FDI's impacts on sustainable development*

The impact assessment under FDIQR principle 1.d refers to multiple processes, all of which can be further strengthened in an IIA context. Such processes include: (i) impact assessment and periodic review of measures of general application (e.g. through the implementation of strategic impact assessment (SIA) processes); (ii) impact assessment of investment projects (e.g. through the implementation of environmental and social impact assessment (ESIA) processes); and (iii) monitoring and evaluation of the effects of the policy or project on sustainable development objectives.

#### *Impact assessment and periodic review of measures of general application*

Several treaties within the IIA sample (e.g. EU-Angola SIFA, Article 25; WTO IFD Agreement, Article 23) address the impact assessment of measures of general application (such as laws, regulations, judicial decisions, and administrative rulings). Article 22.8 of the EU-New Zealand FTA goes a step further by identifying the specific social, economic, and environmental impacts that should be analysed in the impact assessment, in line with the FDIQR principles. It also requires the analysis of the rationale supporting the adoption of relevant measures, including through assessment of potential alternatives. Furthermore, contrary to the EU-Angola SIFA and the WTO IFD Agreement, which only encourage the parties to undertake relevant impact assessments, the requirements under the EU-New Zealand FTA are formulated as binding obligations.

Treaty provisions on the impact assessment of measures of general application are already fully aligned with the FDIQR principles, both from a subject-matter and intensity perspective. States wishing to further strengthen such provisions could draw inspiration from domestic practices on SIA, to the extent that these are compatible with and relevant to their respective jurisdictions. For example, domestic laws may provide for the obligation to explicitly evaluate the impacts of policies, plans, and other measures of general application on specific issues, such as climate change. They could also require that the impact assessment extends to the consideration of the positive contribution of the relevant policy, plan, or measure on specific sustainable development objectives. Depending on their specific objectives and priorities, the parties may incorporate such elements also in the context of relevant IIA provisions on SIA.

The example below considers elements of Article 22.8, EU-New Zealand FTA. It also assumes that negotiating states wish to strengthen impact assessment provisions by incorporating additional elements to be considered in the context of SIA, in particular from an environmental perspective. Such additional elements might concern, for example, the requirement for the assessment to focus not only on potential adverse impacts of the measure of general application on sustainable development but also the positive contribution they can make.

The example also assumes that negotiating parties wish to strengthen their co-operation to ensure that SIA processes at the domestic level will be effectively implemented, with a view to addressing potential challenges. Relevant joint initiatives may be further identified in the context of the IIA-based joint committee, and may entail, among others, activities aimed at the exchange of information and best practices on SIA implementation, as well as technical assistance and capacity building programmes seeking to strengthen governmental capacity to correctly implement SIA processes. The joint committee can also further identify opportunities to harness the support of development co-operation or international organisations operating in the field.

### Impact assessment on measures of general application

1. The regulatory authority of each Party affirms its intention to carry out, in accordance with its respective rules and procedures, an impact assessment of major regulatory measures it is preparing.

2. For carrying out an impact assessment, the regulatory authority of each Party shall promote the identification and consideration of: (a) the need for a regulatory measure, including the nature and the significance of the problem a regulatory measure intends to address; (b) any feasible and appropriate regulatory and non-regulatory options that would achieve the Party's public policy objectives, including the option of not regulating; (c) to the extent possible and relevant, the potential social, economic and environmental impact of the options, such as any impacts on ***climate change, biodiversity, land, soil, water and air, population and human health, labour rights***, international trade and investment, the impact on SMEs, ***and gender***; (d) ***the positive contribution of the proposed measures to sustainable development, including decarbonisation, labour rights, population and human health, and gender equality; and (e)*** how the options under consideration relate to relevant international standards, if any, including the reason for any divergence, where appropriate.

3. With respect to any impact assessment that a regulatory authority of a Party has carried out for a regulatory measure, that regulatory authority shall report on the factors it considered in its assessment and summarise the relevant findings. The information shall be made publicly available no later than when the regulatory measure to which it relates is made publicly available.

**4. *The Parties shall strengthen their co-operation in the domestic implementation of processes aimed at assessing the impact of major measures of general application on sustainable development.***

Source: The provision above is based on Article 22.8, EU-New Zealand FTA. The wording in bold is an example of text that – depending on the context, objectives and level of ambition of treaty parties – state parties could introduce in their IIAs, in alignment with the FDIQR principles and to incorporate developments from domestic practices relevant to their respective jurisdictions.

#### *Periodic review of measures of general application*

Provisions on periodic review of measures of general application are included in the EU-Angola SIFA and the WTO IFD Agreement, in both cases drafted in exhortative and high-level terms. Binding language appears, instead, in Article 22.9 of the EU-New Zealand FTA, which provides both for the criteria guiding the review exercise and the transparency requirements applicable to the process, in line with the FDIQR.

The example below considers elements of the EU-New Zealand FTA as drafting reference. Also in this case, it considers a scenario where the parties wish to address the issue of domestic implementation by relying on their co-operation, identifying initiatives that contribute to strengthening domestic capacity in undertaking periodic review processes.

### Periodic review of measures of general application

1. The regulatory authority of each Party shall maintain processes or mechanisms to promote periodic review of regulatory measures in effect.

2. The regulatory authority of each Party shall endeavour to ensure that periodic reviews consider, where appropriate: (a) whether there are opportunities to achieve its public policy objectives more effectively and efficiently; and (b) whether the regulatory measures under review are likely to remain fit for purpose.

3. The regulatory authority of each Party shall, to the extent possible and appropriate, make publicly available any plans for, and the results of, such periodic review.

***4. The Parties shall strengthen their co-operation in the domestic implementation of processes aimed at periodically review the impact of major measures of general application on sustainable development.***

Source: The provision above is based on Article 22.9, EU-New Zealand FTA. The wording in bold is an example of text that – depending on the context, objectives and level of ambition of treaty parties – state parties could include in their IIAs, in alignment with the FDIQR principles.

*Impact assessment of investment projects*

In the IIA sample, language on environmental and social impact assessment (ESIA), ESIA only appears in the EU-New Zealand FTA, exclusively in the context of activities related to the production of energy goods and raw materials. The review of domestic practices on ESIA however, may provide inspiration to negotiating parties wishing to strengthen this provision in alignment with the FDIQR.

The example below takes Article 13.8, EU-New Zealand FTA as starting point for negotiating parties wishing to extend its scope beyond the energy sector. A potential approach could be to make the relevant treaty language general in scope, as the ESIA requirement is not limited to specific sectors of investment. Parties could also expand the scope of the assessment to adverse social impacts to include impacts on labour rights, development of small and medium-sized enterprises, and gender equality, in line with domestic legislation. Lastly, it also provides for the need to consider the positive contribution of the investment to sustainable development, as potentially envisaged under domestic law.

Parties could also include language on co-operation to ensure the correct implementation of the EIA process. As in the SIA case, the joint committee established under the IIA can contribute to the development of initiatives seeking to provide technical assistance and capacity building to government officials, with a view to building their capacity in the implementation of EIA processes. The joint committee could also evaluate how to further take advantage of opportunities offered under development co-operation or the support provided by international organisations in this area.

## Impact assessment of investment projects

1. Each Party shall ensure that its laws and regulations require an environmental and social impact assessment for activities that may have a significant ***social and environmental impact***.

2. Each Party shall: (a) ensure that all interested persons, including NGOs, have an early and effective opportunity, and an appropriate time period, to participate in the EIA as well as an appropriate time period to provide comments on the ESIA report; (b) take into account the findings of the ESIA prior to granting the authorisation; (c) make publicly available the outcome findings of the ESIA; (d) identify and assess as appropriate the significant effects of a project on: (i) population and human health; (ii) biodiversity; (iii) land, soil, water, air and climate; (iv) cultural heritage and landscape; ***(iv) labour rights, SME development and gender equality***; ***and (e) the positive contribution of the proposed measures to sustainable development, including decarbonisation, labour rights, population and human health, and gender equality.***

***4. The Parties shall strengthen their co-operation to support the domestic implementation of environmental and social impact assessment processes.***

Source: The provision above is based on Article 13.8, EU-New Zealand FTA. The wording in bold is an example of text that – depending on the context, objectives and level of ambition of treaty parties – the parties could introduce in their IIAs, in alignment with the FDIQR principles and to incorporate developments from domestic practices relevant to their respective jurisdictions.

### *Monitoring & evaluation*

Contrary to other areas under the FDIQR principle 1.d, monitoring & evaluation over the continuous impacts of investment projects, policies and plans is relatively new in an IIA context. There are currently no provisions in the IIA sample addressing the matter. Moreover, clear parameters guiding monitoring and evaluation are also lacking, both at the international and domestic level.

Given the novelty of the topic, rather than introducing substantive treaty language setting out binding commitments on monitoring and evaluation, parties wishing to address this issue through IIAs could, for example, focus on the development of joint initiatives seeking to strengthen monitoring and evaluation frameworks, including in the context of the activities of national investment promotion agencies (IPAs). Such initiatives could be pursued in the context of treaty-based joint committees, with the support of development co-operation resources and of relevant international organisations. They could include, among others:

- The gathering and sharing of data concerning the impacts of FDI on sustainable development.
- Technical support in the establishment of data tracking tools.
- Technical exchanges and study visits between national evaluation units and IPAs, to facilitate the sharing of best practices on monitoring and evaluation.

If appropriate depending on the context, treaty-based co-operation could be complemented by specific treaty provisions setting out the parties' high-level commitment to work together in this area.

### Monitoring and evaluation

The Parties shall strengthen their co-operation in the design and implementation of effective monitoring and evaluation frameworks, to assess the impacts of FDI, related policies, and major measures of general application on sustainable development.

Source: The provision above is an example of text that – depending on the context, objectives and level of ambition of treaty parties – the parties could introduce in their IIAs, in alignment with the FDIQR principles.

### *5.2.2. FDIQR principle 2.b: Policy coherence between gender and investment priorities*

IIAs can contribute to strengthening policy coherence between gender and investment objectives, in line with FDIQR principle 2.b. To this end, parties may introduce specific treaty language setting out their commitment to uphold both values in a manner that is conducive to their meaningful fulfilment. This type of language is already present – in hortatory or declaratory terms – in several treaties within the IIA sample, including the EU-Angola SIFA, the Chile-Canada FTA, and the EU-New Zealand FTA.

Building on Article 35, EU-Angola SIFA, the example below addresses a scenario where state parties wish to create binding "best effort" obligations in this area. The example first recognises existing linkages between gender and investment-related objectives. It then strengthens the intensity of existing provisions by introducing an obligation for the parties to ensure alignment between objectives in the two areas.

### Investment and gender

The Parties recognise that inclusive investment policies can contribute to advancing women's economic empowerment and gender equality, in line with Sustainable Development Goal 5 of the UN2030 Agenda. They acknowledge the important contribution by women to economic growth through their participation in economic activity, including investment. The Parties endeavour to implement this Agreement in a manner that promotes and enhances gender equality.

Source: The provision above is based on Article 35, EU-Angola SIFA.

Negotiating parties, however, might deem that reliance on a treaty obligation reconciling gender and investment objectives alone is insufficient to achieve the desired purpose. Co-operation in this area plays a key role and can draw from the FDIQR to provide more specific guidance on activities that would allow the parties to achieve policy coherence, while also contributing to additional FDIQR principles addressing gender equality. Relevant activities could include, for example:

- Regulatory co-operation seeking to remove barriers preventing women's full participation in trade and investment opportunities.
- Capacity building and exchanges of best practices on how to draft gender-aligned investment laws and policies.
- Implementation of programmes to link women with the opportunities created by foreign investors (e.g. matchmaking events, supplier diversity programmes, education campaigns).
- Coaching and mentoring programmes seeking to develop women's professional skills in sectors target of FDI.

### 5.2.3. FDIQR principle 4.a: Awareness raising on FDI's contribution to sustainable development

Within the IIA sample, the consideration of initiatives on awareness raising on the contribution of FDI to sustainable development looks at two specific areas: gender and decarbonisation.

#### *Awareness raising on FDI's contribution to gender equality*

Concerning gender, awareness raising provisions appear in the EU-New Zealand FTA and the Chile-Canada FTA. In both cases, their scope is limited to increasing the public knowledge of gender equality laws, regulations, and policies. The analysis of domestic practices, however, has highlighted how awareness raising can extend to a wide range of initiatives seeking to sensitise women and girls on the benefits that FDI creates for them, including with respect to job creation. Treaty parties to which such domestic practices are relevant may wish to take these additional elements into account in their IIA negotiation efforts. To broaden the scope of awareness raising provisions, it could be possible to rely on a combination of substantive treaty language and parties' co-operation.

The example below considers elements of Article Nbis-01, para 7 of the Chile-Canada FTA by providing for the parties' obligation to co-operate to raise awareness on the opportunities that the Treaty creates for women and girls.

#### Awareness raising on FDI's impacts on gender equality

1. Each Party shall co-operate to promote public awareness of the economic opportunities that [the Treaty] creates for women and girls.

2. Each Party shall promote public awareness and transparency of its gender equality laws, regulations, policies and practices.

Source: The provision above is based on Article Nbis-01, para 7, Chile-Canada FTA.

If established under the relevant treaty, parties can harness existing implementation mechanisms – including the joint committees established under the applicable IIA – to identify potential initiatives that they can jointly pursue in this area. These can include, among others:

- Public information and education campaigns seeking to encourage women and girls to access professional and educational opportunities in sectors that are target of FDI.
- Community-based initiatives, such as public meetings or dialogue platforms, seeking to sensitise stakeholders on the challenges that women and girls face in accessing economic opportunities.
- Trainings for public officials and private sector members designed to combat persisting gender stereotypes.
- Initiatives and programmes seeking to close the gender gap in selected priority sectors, with a view to achieving 50/50 employment between men and women.

While these initiatives have mostly domestic relevance, parties' co-operation may ultimately facilitate the exchange of information, best practices and lessons learned, further contributing to the implementation of international commitments.

*Awareness raising on FDI's contribution to decarbonisation*

As for decarbonisation, there are currently no provisions in the IIA sample regulating awareness raising in this area. An implicit reference appears only in the Singapore-Australia GEA when addressing the parties' co-operation with ecolabelling organisation. Given the relative novelty of the topic, an effort to strengthen IIAs' alignment with FDIQR principles on awareness raising rests mostly on enhancing the parties' co-operation. These efforts could be performed in the implementation of existing IIA sample provisions such as Article 32, para 3 EU-Angola SIFA, which calls on the parties to "work together to strengthen their co-operation on investment-related aspects of climate change policies and measures bilaterally, regionally and in international fora".

By relying on treaty-based joint committees and harnessing development co-operation, parties could focus on the design and implementation of initiatives seeking to sensitise consumers and influence their behaviour in a way that supports decarbonisation efforts. Such initiatives could include, among others, the implementation of sensibilisation campaigns seeking to influence individual patterns of consumption and information campaigns on energy efficiency and the availability and application of ecolabelling schemes.

### 5.2.4. FDIQR principle 4.b and principle 4.c: Investment promotion and facilitation

Most treaties within the IIA sample consider investment promotion and facilitation activities jointly. This is the approach adopted, for example, in the Investment Protocol to the AfCFTA, the EU-New Zealand FTA and the EU-Angola SIFA. All these agreements first identify the priority sectors for investment promotion and facilitation. Attention is mostly placed on sectors that can contribute to climate objectives. These include, among others: investments in climate change mitigation and adaptation projects, investment in environmental goods and services; investment in nature-based solutions; or investment in specific sectors such as renewable energy, low-carbon technologies, raw materials, sustainable agriculture, green infrastructure.

One option available to parties wishing to strengthen the linkage between investment promotion and facilitation activities and sustainable development could be to build on the language already found in the IIA sample to broaden the list of target priority sectors. In practice, the choice of sectors is context-specific and will depend on the parties' own priorities and choices. Examples of sustainable development-related sectors in alignment with the FDIQR include, among others:

- Gender equality: e.g. investment in women-led businesses; investment in companies with strong gender equality focus, including in terms of percentage of women employed; investment in sectors that can provide key support services to women, enabling them to benefit from the economic opportunities arising from FDI (e.g. transportation, healthcare, technology, and digitalisation).
- Productivity and Innovation: e.g. investment in research, development, and innovation in areas with high potential for productivity and innovation, such as renewable energy and clean technologies, raw materials, manufacturing in technology and IT services, pharmaceuticals, financial services and financial technology, logistics, communications.

In limited instances, IIAs also identify examples of what promotion and facilitation activities entail. Parties could include an interpretative provision listing examples of investment promotion and facilitation activities. Such an approach, which is not prescriptive in nature, would still provide parties with enough flexibility to decide which investment promotion or facilitation initiatives are the most appropriate depending on the context and the specific objectives pursued.

### Investment promotion and facilitation for sustainable development

1. Each Party shall promote and facilitate investments in:

   - [To be completed with a list of sectors relevant for the achievement of sustainable development objectives, based on the parties' interests and priorities.]

2. By way of example, promotion and facilitation activities may include:

   - [To be completed with list of activities, based on selected priority sectors for sustainable development.]

Source: The provision above is based on Articles 6 and 7, Investment Protocol to the AfCFTA; Article 19.11, paras 4-5, EU-New Zealand FTA; Article 33, EU-Angola SIFA.

Certain treaty provisions address specific investment facilitation measures in more specific terms. IIAs such as the EU-Angola SIFA and the WTO IFD Agreement specifically encourage the parties to establish domestic supplier databases, as a way to facilitate linkages between foreign investors and domestic firms. Relevant provisions are mostly drafted in hortatory terms, without establishing any binding commitments for the parties, thus allowing parties to retain flexibility on the modalities and timeline for implementation of such type of commitment.

### Linkages with domestic suppliers

Each Party is encouraged to make available to investors and persons seeking to invest information on possible relevant domestic suppliers, including micro, small and medium-sized enterprises and women-led enterprises.

Source: The provision above is based on Article 24, WTO IFD Agreement; Article 11, EU-Angola SIFA.

Regardless of any language, the parties can rely on co-operation for the development of joint investment promotion and facilitation initiatives. Investment promotion activities could consist of, for example:

- Exchanging information on metrics, scoring mechanisms and approaches used by investment promotion agencies to target, measure and monitor sustainable investment.
- Organising joint investment promotion activities in priority sectors, including conferences and seminars, business fora, and fairs.
- Exchange of information and best practices for the development and implementation of policy and legal frameworks conducive to the achievement of sustainable development-related objectives (e.g. promotion of low carbon investments, improved access to finance and digital technology for women, promotion of supply chain development and SME absorptive capacity).

As for investment facilitation activities, these can include, among others:

- Establishing green corridors or green one-stop-shops seeking to ease administrative procedures in connection with low carbon investments.
- Providing advisory services seeking to enhance the sustainability profile of both foreign investors and domestic suppliers operating in priority sectors.
- Establishing suppliers databases showcasing women-led businesses or domestic businesses responding to specific sustainability-related criteria (e.g. using low carbon technologies).

- Providing matchmaking and networking events to promote the establishment of linkages between the foreign investor and, e.g. low carbon domestic suppliers, partners and distributors, or women-led businesses.
- Establishing and implementing supplier development programmes and skills development programmes to build the capabilities of domestic suppliers and local workforce in areas of interest for foreign investors, e.g. low carbon technologies and practices.
- Establishing and implementing skills development programmes, seeking to enhance linkages between foreign investors and women entrepreneurs in the host state.

### *5.2.5. FDIQR principle 4.e: Promoting the consideration of ESG criteria in investment decisions*

FDIQR principle 4.e addresses the importance of considering environmental, social and governance (ESG) criteria when taking investment decisions. The only treaty within the IIA sample that addresses ESG is the Singapore-Australia GEA. This treaty provides a framework for the parties' co-operation in two different but related areas: the strengthening of ESG ecosystems in the parties' respective countries, and the development of robust global climate-related financial disclosures and reporting standards. Co-operation in both areas is especially important, as it contributes to addressing some of the main shortcomings that affect the uptake and application of ESG standards. These relate to, among others, inconsistencies in the construction of ESG ratings, difficulties in data comparability and the general fragmentation of the ESG environment.

One option available to parties wishing to harness their IIAs to strengthen their domestic ESG ecosystems could be to create a common framework for collaboration. For example, they could use the IIA to clarify their intention to co-operate to improve their own domestic frameworks on ESG disclosure. The adoption of a soft language is justified due to the many uncertainties that still surround ESG as a topic. Additionally, or in alternative, the parties could consider introducing a binding obligation to work together for the development of ESG metrics suitable to provide comparable and consistent criteria for non-financial disclosure, thus facilitating investment decisions. What co-operation will entail in practice can be then determined on a case-by-case basis.

#### Strengthening ESG frameworks

1. State parties are encouraged to improve their legal and regulatory framework on ESG, with a view to improving decision making by investors.

2. For this purpose, state parties shall work together to facilitate the development and uptake of consistent, comparable, and robust ESG metrics and standards, with a view to improving disclosure of non-financial information.

Source: The provision above is based on paragraph 9.c.viii, Singapore-Australia GEA.

## 5.3. Areas for future research

Recent IIAs are increasingly incorporating provisions designed to facilitate sustainable investment. While these mostly focus on traditional facilitation measures (e.g. transparency, streamlining of administrative processes), the review carried out in the previous chapters shows that IIAs are also starting to incorporate provisions with a broader scope, aimed at improving the investment environment in the host state for the purpose of harnessing sustainable investment.

This chapter has analysed how such provisions can be further strengthened in alignment with the principles of the FDIQR in selected areas. The approach identified rests on a combination of sample language based on existing treaties – with potential amendments based on the review of domestic practices in selected OECD and non-OECD countries – and parties' co-operation in the context of treaty-based mechanisms. By themselves, however, these tools might not necessarily lead to increased sustainable investment. Domestic implementation of IIAs commitments on sustainable investment remains a necessary precondition. Currently, there is no consensus as to what domestic implementation means. The framework developed under the previous chapters, relying not only on parties' co-operation but also on international organisations' support and development co-operation, can however be harnessed to strengthen domestic implementation efforts.

It is also important to stress that new commitments on sustainable investment are not the only type of sustainable development-related provisions appearing in IIAs. Traditional IIA provisions, addressing issues such as expropriation or fair and equitable treatment, may also incorporate sustainable development-related concerns.

Such provisions raise different sets of issues, both in terms of treaty language and in terms of implementation. Concerning the first issue, research has been ongoing in international fora – including, but not limited, to the OECD – to determine how to align investment treaty language with sustainable development objectives, for example looking at issues relating to the preservation of policy space for the host state. On the second issue, future research could similarly explore the role of the proposed implementation framework, based on parties' co-operation, international organisations' support and development co-operation, to further strengthen implementation of these different categories of investment treaty provisions.

www.ingramcontent.com/pod-product-compliance
Lightning Source LLC
Chambersburg PA
CBHW061223240926
51846CB00006B/1325